SOUND THEOLOGY

A Reader

WORSHIP AND WITNESS

The Worship and Witness series seeks to foster a rich, interdisciplinary conversation on the theology and practice of public worship, a conversation that will be integrative and expansive. Integrative, in that scholars and practitioners from a wide range of disciplines and ecclesial contexts will contribute studies that engage church and academy. Expansive, in that the series will engage voices from the global church and foreground crucial areas of inquiry for the vitality of public worship in the twenty-first century.

The Worship and Witness series demonstrates and cultivates the interaction of topics in worship studies with a range of crucial questions, topics, and insights drawn from other fields. These include the traditional disciplines of theology, history, and pastoral ministry—as well as cultural studies, political theology, spirituality, and music and the arts. The series focus will thus bridge church worship practices and the vital witness these practices nourish.

We are pleased that you have chosen to join us in this conversation, and we look forward to sharing this learning journey with you.

SERIES EDITORS:

John D. Witvliet
Noel Snyder
Maria Cornou

SOUND THEOLOGY

Pipe Organ Power Plays among Protestants, Pulpits, Professors, and Peers

A Reader

Compiled by
Randall Dean Engle

CASCADE *Books* · Eugene, Oregon

SOUND THEOLOGY: PIPE ORGAN POWER PLAYS AMONG PROTESTANTS, PULPITS, PROFESSORS, AND PEERS
A Reader

Copyright © 2025 Randall Dean Engle. All rights reserved. Except for brief quotations in critical publications or reviews, no part of this book may be reproduced in any manner without prior written permission from the publisher. Write: Permissions, Wipf and Stock Publishers, 199 W. 8th Ave., Suite 3, Eugene, OR 97401.

Cascade Books
An Imprint of Wipf and Stock Publishers
199 W. 8th Ave., Suite 3
Eugene, OR 97401

www.wipfandstock.com

PAPERBACK ISBN: 978-1-6667-1733-4
HARDCOVER ISBN: 978-1-6667-1734-1
EBOOK ISBN: 978-1-6667-1735-8

Cataloguing-in-Publication data:

Names: Engle, Randall Dean, editor.

Title: Sound theology : pipe organ power plays among Protestants, pulpits, professors, and peers: a reader / Edited by Randall Dean Engle.

Description: Eugene, OR: Cascade Books, 2025 | Series: Worship and Witness | Includes bibliographical references and index.

Identifiers: ISBN 978-1-6667-1733-4 (paperback) | ISBN 978-1-6667-1734-1 (hardcover) | ISBN 978-1-6667-1735-8 (ebook)

Subjects: LCSH: Organ (musical instrument)—Europe. | Organ (musical instrument)—History. | Church music.

Classification: ML553 E54 2025 (paperback) | ML553 (ebook)

01/27/25

For Kathy
Res pulchra est gaudium in æternum.

CONTENTS

Preface ix

1 | Professors

Johannes Molanus: *De Organista* (1587) 3

Rodolpho Hospiniano: *On the Origin of Organs in Churches* (1603) 9

André Rivet: *Prologomena to the Psalms* (excerpt, 1626) 16

Gisbertus Voetius: *Letter to Constantijn Huygens* (1641) 19

Ionnes Heimenbergius and Gisbertus Voetius: *The Organ and Organ Music*, part 1 (1641, 1661) 21

Gisbertus Voetius: *Appendix Apologetica* (1661) 64

Martin Schook: *Organ Music in Churches* (1663) 68

Gilbertus Voetius, Andreas Essenius, and Matthias Nethenus: *Theological Advice* (1655) 97

2 | People

Jean-Etienne Duranti: *De ritibus Ecclesiae cath[olicae]*, chapter XIII: *De organis* (1591) 103

Council of Sneek: *Terms and Conditions for a new Organist* (1602) 106

Jan Jansz. Calckman: *Antidotum* (excerpt, 1641) 108

CONTENTS

Abcoude: *Request to magistrates to cease organ music in the churches* (1649) 111

Conventikel of The Hague: *Petition to the Church Council of The Hague* (1642) 114

3 | Pastors

Andreas Osiander: *Commentary on Psalm 150* (excerpt, 1524) 121

Hermannum Faukeel: *Marriage song sung to the glory of Jesus Christ* (1628) 122

Christoph Frick: *Prayer of Dedication for the new Organ in Bardowick* (1631) 126

Christophilus Eubulus [Jacobus Koelman]: *The Matters Necessary for Reformation* (1678) 128

Abraham van de Velde: *The Wonders of the Most High* (excerpt, 1733) 131

Ægidius Francken: *Conclusion of sermon on Psalm 150:3-4* (1734) 133

Bibliography 135

Subject Index 143

Scripture Index 149

PREFACE

Translations are both a maddening and an addicting task. Maddening because the reader needs to grasp in contemporary English what was meant by the author, but the translator cannot rewrite the author. Accordingly, do you break up the run-on sentence? Do you replace an anachronistic verb with a contemporary replacement? Do you let vulgar language stand? What about unknown clichés or turns of phrase—substitute modern equivalents? Is it necessary to transcribe all the Latin ligature markings even when they don't make sense? But in the end, the work is addicting because the result can be illuminating.

To stay on the fulcrum, here's what I've done. First, I did an honest translation without much scrubbing or sanitizing except to render the texts in modern grammatical English. Second, I employed every convenience for the reader I wish I had had: spelled out abbreviations, gave full names and dates of authors, and footnoted extant references. Third (and this is important), the first time an author is referenced in this *Reader* (across entries) they are annotated and footnoted. If they are referenced again, I spare the reader a replicate footnote—to do so would have turned this little primer into a twelve-volume encyclopedia set.

I hope it's like this: Say you want to visit a vintage Victorian home. You're excited to see the carved newel post on the stairs, the busy wallpaper, the intricate fretwork, and the period brass. At the same time, you don't want to fall through creaky wooden floors; it's okay to bolster them. And while you're at it, would it hurt to level the front porch, polish the brass, and dry out the cellar? This is how to approach these quirky, wondrous literary gems of the past. They're cleaned up, accessible, and safe, yet remain products of their time. I know you'll enjoy the visit.

Fourth, and most importantly. I am not a natural linguist. I am thankful for all those who God put in my life who have shared generously of their skill and time for this project (and then shared again, and yet again). People like Nancy van Baak, Raymond Blacketer, John Exalto, David van Dyke, Jan Hofstee, Michael Krogh, and Mark Williams. This work is really theirs. But I'll take the onus for mistakes.

I am so pleased that for the first time, really, English readers have access to great theological writing of the sixteenth and seventeenth centuries in regard to church music and pipe organ use. During the reformations, storms erupted over the Roman Catholic Church, indulgences, Arminianism, and the like, but it is often a surprise for many to discover how much attention was also given to liturgical matters in general, and to the pipe organ in specific. It's also striking how much holy wisdom is here for the contemporary church.

Welcome to the Reformation debate over pipe organ use or nonuse. Professors, preachers, and politicians are waiting to speak from their respective podiums, pulpits, and pews. They ask to be heard.

1

Professors

JOHANNES MOLANUS

De Organista (1587)

Johannes Molanus (Jan Vermeulen, 1533–1585) was an influential Counter-Reformation Flemish theologian of Louvain University, where he was professor of theology and rector from 1578. From 1561 to 1563 he was headmaster at the Latin School in Duisburg. Born at Lille, he was a priest and canon of Saint Peter's Church in Louvain, where he died in 1585. Molanus shows that the organ controversy was not limited to the first and second-generation Reformed. As a Roman Catholic, he shares his concern that the organ's provenance is pagan, that organ use smacks of Judaism, and that a bravura organist would "exhaust the audience with excessive wind to show off his art."

Johannes Molani. *De canonici libri tres: I. De canoniorum vita. II. De eorum officijs. III. De dominio canonicorum & seruis ecclesiarum. Item, Orationes tres, De agnis Dei, De decimis dandis, De decimis defendendis cum trib. indicibus.* **Coloniæ: Birckman, 1587, 214–16:**

CHAPTER 40
THE ORGANIST

One can observe that an organist, commonly called, may be numbered with the musicians. However, all musical instruments are called organs, as is noted by the grammarians, because of their excellence but by custom now these instruments are called organs because they are inflated by bellows. Already once Saint Augustine noted this, writing on the Psalms: *All musical instruments are called* organs *not only because they are big and inflated with bellows.* And again, on the passage "Praise him with strings and the organ," *"organ" is the general name of all musical instruments, although now the general custom holds that those instruments that are inflated by bellows are properly called organs: but what type of instrument is signified here I do not judge. For although* organ *is a Greek term generally applied to all musical instruments, this one, which is blown with bellows, the Greeks call by another name. It is the common custom, however, that it be called an* organ *more in Latin as customarily used.*[1]

In the naming of all things, this instrument which sounds through the service of wind is called as *pneumatic organ* by Vitruvius,[2] but no Greek name is suggested. Others, skilled in Greek, would say how the instrument is called in Greece. Nor is it true that that famous and magnificent instrument, which in Latin custom is called an organ through the use of an epithet, lacks its own name among the eloquent Greeks, especially since already once among the Africans the divine Augustine wrote that it was called by another name by the Greeks themselves, because then indeed the art of building organs came from the Greeks to us. For this musical instrument first began in France, as an imitation of the Greeks, through the initiative of a certain Georgius, and with the aid of the emperor Louis. For this we have as witness Aimonius, the Parisian historian, a monk of Saint Germain who made clear at those times that *Count Baldric, the prefect of the Pannonian border, presented to his lord emperor a certain presbyter, Georgius by name, a man of upright life, who promised that he could build an organ after the manner of the Greeks. The emperor graciously received him and, because God had placed him over that nation which before himself had not usually been considered a kingdom of the Franks, gave him thanks and*

---

1. Aurelius Augustine (354–430), *Ennarrationes* 5:302: *Organum autem generale nomen est omnium vasorum musicorum, quamvis iam obtinuerit consuetudo ut organa proprie dicantur ea quae inflantur follibus: quod genus significatum hic esse non arbitror. Nam cum organum vocabulum graecum sit, ut dixi, generale omnibus musicis instrumentis, hoc cui folles adhibentur, alio Graeci nomine appellant. Ut autem organum dicatur, magis Latina et ea vulgaris est consuetudo. Quod ergo ait: IN CHORDIS ET ORGANO, videtur mihi aliquod organum quod chordas habeat, significare voluisse.*

2. = Marcus Vitruvius Pollio (80–15 BC). Vitruvius is the author of *De architectura*, known today as *The Ten Books on Architecture*, a treatise on architecture dedicated to the emperor Augustus. See *Marci Vitruvii Pollionis De architectura*.

commended him to Talculf [of Thuringia], *the overseer of the sacred chests. He ordered him to be maintained at public expense, and mandated that he prepare whatever things should be necessary to this work.*³

Although already before from the donation of the emperor Constantine organs came to King Pepin in Compiègne while he was marking the general convention.

I believe, however, that the most Christian princes quickly transferred organs, which until then had been unused among them and for which they gave thanks to God, to the use of ecclesiastical office, following the example of the holy fathers. Therefore it is read in the provincial synod of Siena: *The church accepts the use* of organs *for divine worship and service.*⁴ But by which fathers? The bishop of Mende, William Durant, explained this already three hundred years ago. For in treating the hymn which today is placed in the preface to the sacrifice of the mass, he said *in this concord of angels and men, whenever the instruments sound together, what was introduced by David and Solomon, who taught that hymns should be sung in the sacrifices of the Lord with organs and other musical instruments, and that praises should be exclaimed by the people.*⁵

But Durant wrote his *Rationale of the Divine Offices* at the same time as or a little before that when Saint Thomas Aquinas wrote his *Summa Theologiae*. Even though the holy Doctor somewhere in his *Summa* says by way of objection that musical instruments, like cithers, and psaltry ought not to be taken up in church in divine praise lest people be seen to Judaize, still I think that he did not ignore that which was cited from Durant, but that in his words he signified that the use of organs in his time had not been received in the church universally, even if organs were being played in some particular churches then for the sacrifice of the masses.

---

3. = Aimonus Floriacensis (Aimoin of Fleury, 965–1008), *Historiae Francorum*, 4:64:520–30: *Adduxit verò Baldricus domino imperatori presbyterum quendam, Georgium nomine, bonæ vitæ hominem, qui se promitteret organum more posse Græcorum componere. Quê imperator gratanter suscepit: & quia Deus illi, quæ ante se inusitata crāt regno Francorum, attribuebat, gratiarum actiones reddidit, ac Tanculfo sacrorum scriniorum prælato commendavit, publicisque stipendiis curare iussit, & e quae huic operi necessaria sorent præparare mandavit.*

4. Council of Senonense, 1526–1528. Mansi, *Sacrorum* conciliorum, 32:17:1190: *Organorum usum ecclesia à Patribus ad cultum servitiumque Divinum recepit.*

5. = Guilelmus Durantis (1230–1296), *Rationale Divinorum*, III:100: *Sane in hoc Angelorum & hominum concêntu, quãndoque organa conceperant, q, à David & à Salomone introductum est. qui instituerunt hymnos in sacrificio Domini organis, & aliis instrumentis musicis concrepari, & laudes à populo conclamari.*

But now, says Navarre,[6] the music of organs has been received and prescribed in the entire Christian church by custom, which because of the aforementioned respect can be called rational, even if their sound should not be valued as highly as the crowd values it, thinking that God is not decently served where there are no organs. For although it may be a little advantageous to imperfect and uneducated Christians, for exciting them

---

6. = Martin Aspilcueta (1493–1586), *Enchiridion*, 16:53: *Multi (eius verba sunt) organistæ faciant sonare sæpius organo cantiones profanas in ecclesiis, imo & vanas, & quandoque malas; cuiusmodi sunt, quas vocant baxas, & Altas, & alias cantilenas, quas vulgus novit esse turpes, obscoenas, & petulantes: quod palam est peccatum, præsertim cum id faciunt, quando officia divina siunt, tam ob irreventiam, quæ loco sacro sit, quam propter occasionem, quæ præbetur avertendi mentes ab attentione rerum divinarum & spiritualium, & ad intendendum easdem temporalibus, vanis, & malis. Tum quia est causa, quod multis in locis non canuntur, nec audiuntur* Credo, *&* Gloria *a populo in festis, quibus non iubetur cani, ut pro his audiantur fistulæ, & harmoniæ; sed ut animo & ore confiteamur sanctam fidem catholicam, & ut lassant Domino ob suum adventum agamus. Tum quia multi organistae, quo suam artem ostentent, & plene audiantur, tamdiu pulsant (cum tamen ille pulsus non sit aliud, quam, ut ille ait, sine mente sonus) ut nonnunquam Missam una hora diutius æquo protrahant: quare adeo audientes lassant, ut cum devenitur ad id, quod plurimum importat, puta concionem, aut contemplationem passionis Redemtoris, & redemtionis humani generis, quæ repræsentantur in sanctissima illa consecratione, tam sunt sastidisi, ut plus cogitent de egressu ecclesiæ quam de illis mysteriis. Tum quia datur occasio, ut interim, dum organa sonant, qui in choro sunt, colloquantur, iocentur, rideant, negocientur, quandoque paullo plus cogitent de eo, quod organa sonant, quam eorum fistulæ cogitant de eo, quod ipsi agunt vel dicunt.* Many organists frequently play profane, and even vain and sometimes evil songs in the church on the organ; of this sort are the ones they call *baxas*, [music for soft instruments], and *atlas* [music for loud instruments], and other songs that the people know to be filthy, obscene, and wanton. This is clearly sin, especially when they do this during the divine offices, because of irreverence in a holy place, and just as much because of the occasion it may present for diverting minds from their attention to divine and spiritual things and bending them toward temporal, vain, and evil things. For this reason, in many places the *Credo* and *Gloria* are neither sung nor heard by the people on feast days, on which these are commanded to be sung—and not indeed so that, instead of them, the pipes and the harmonies may be heard, but so that we may confess with heart and mouth the holy Catholic faith, and so that we may give thanks to the Lord for his coming. Moreover, many organists, that they may display their skill and may be heard more fully, pound the keys so long (though this pounding is no more than what has been called mindless sound) that sometimes the Mass is equally drawn out to longer than an hour. Because of this, the hearers become tired, and when the service gets to a most important point, for example the sermon, the contemplation of the Redeemer's passion, and the redemption of humankind which is presented in that most holy consecration, they are so annoyed that they think more about getting out of church than about those mysteries. Moreover, while the organs play, occasion is given for those in the choir to converse, joke, laugh, and carry on business; whenever they may think a little more on what the organs are playing, they think rather of the pipes than of what they themselves are doing or saying.

to devotion (albeit from afar), still, for those learned and well-founded in Christianity, organ music commonly does them harm by depriving them of the understanding of words, which excite and increase devotion far more effectively. Nevertheless, Cajetan, Cardinal of Sisto, thought that the use of organs could be tolerated because of the alienation of many from divine worship, so that they might be attracted to and take part in divine worship. Still the church never uses them before the Roman pontiff,[7] showing that their use in church is new, or at least not entirely ancient, as is gathered from the 107th question to the Orthodox which exists in Justin [Martyr],[8] and from Navarre, later called Cardinal.

It seems that a third reason can also be added. For the cathedral church of Liège and certain others think to look to the magnificence and honor of their churches, because they have music, from the universal customary use of organs or alternately[9] from either side.

7. = Tommaso de Vio Cajetan (1469–1534), *Summula Caietani*, 227: *Organorum usus in ecclesia licet sit novus (in cuius signum Ecclesia Romana adhuc non utitur eis coram Pontifice) licitus tamen est pro carnalibus adhuc fidelibus & imperfectis*. Cajetan (from his birth place, Gaeta), known as a philosopher and interpreter of Thomas Aquinas, dropped his philosophical studies in order to write a series of biblical commentaries that would demonstrate to Protestants and Catholics alike that the literal sense of the Bible supports Roman Catholic theology.

8. Quæstio 107. *Si ab iis quià vera religione abhorrent, fallendi studio inuenta sunt carmina & cantica, ijs autem qui lege tenentur, inducta sunt propter mentis infantiam, cur ij qui gratiæ perfecta munera & ab ijs modis qui expositi sunt, aliena acceperunt, in templis eorū imitatione qui in lege pueri sunt & infantes, canticis usi sunt?* Explicatio. *Canere non omnino pueros decet, sed canere cum inanimis instrumentis & cum saltatione & crotalis. Itaque ex templis explosus est & sablatus usus instrumentorum eius generis, aliorúmque quæ pueris digna sunt, relictúsque est & retentus cantus omnio. Mouet enim animū ad ardenté cupidataté eius rei, quæ in cantibus delectat sedat motus qui ex carne excitāntur: cogitationes vitiosas, quę ab hostibus qui non cernūtur inferūtur, depellit: irrigat animum ad ferendum fructum diainorum bonorum: fortes ad patientiá in adversis rebus religionis cultores atque pugiles efficit: pijs curationem adhibet molestiarum quæ in rebus ad mundum pertinentibus versantur. Hoc Paulus gladium Spiritus nominanit, quo adversus hostes qui nō vidétut accingit & armat milites veræ religionis. Dei enim verbum est, quod dum & cogitatur & canitur & resonat, dęmones fundit & fugat. * vim habent perficiendi animum virtutibus religioni confentaneis, dum canticis ecclesiasticis in religionis cultoribus oriuntur.* Justino, *Beati Iustini philosophi*, 60–61.

9. *Alternatim*, a technique of liturgical musical performance where a hymn, canticle, or some portion of the Ordinary of the Mass (such as the *Kyrie* and the *Gloria*) would be divided into versets. Each verset would be performed antiphonally by different forces. When plainsong and organ passages alternated, organ music took the place of those parts of the text, so they were never actually spoken during the service. The organ music was often an improvisation on the plainchant used by the singers.

1 | PROFESSORS

So that I may finish with the organist, with a brief admonition to him, first let him remember that the Council of Trent mandated to those in orders that they forbid these kinds of music from their churches, where anything lascivious or impure be mixed with the organ music or song.[10] Finally he should know that it is condemned in various synodical constitutions as an abuse, that many organists often cut short the sacrifice of the mass by interrupting it, which is the confession of our faith, by not singing all the way to the end, and because they prevent the preface and the Lord's prayer to be sung by the priest, hastening as they do to the end of the Mass. Finally, he should remember to praise the Lord through the organ and to excite the audience to devotion to and praise of God, but not to exhaust the audience with excessive wind or to show off his art.

---

10. = Concilium Tridentinum (1545–1563). Church music was dealt with under the *Abuses in the Sacrifice of the Mass* in the Session of the committee on September 10, 1562, in Canon 8. See *Acta Concilii Tridentini: Ab ecclesiis vero musicas eas, ubi, sive organo sive cantu lascivum aut impurum aliquid miscetur, item saeculares omnes actiones, vana atque adeo profana colloquia, deambulationes, strepitus, clamores arceant, ut domus Dei vere domus orationis esse videatur ac dici posit*. Let them keep from the churches those forms of music in which there is mingled, either by the organ or by singing, anything lewd or shameful; also all worldly actions [*saeculares actiones*], as well as vain and indeed profane conversations [*profana colloquia*], walking about, noise [*strepitus*], shouting [*clamores*], so that the House of God may truly be seen both to be, and to be called, a house of prayer.

In the preparatory canon, number 8, of September 10, 1562, which referred to the celebration of Mass in general, and from which the material of canon 9 was eventually derived, we find these words used to refer not to the musicians but to the celebrant: *Sacerdotes, dum missarum sollemnia agunt . . . caveant etiam, ne ita submissa voce verba proferant, ut non commode ab aliis intelligantur, sic tamen, ne clamoroso vocis strepitu audientium fervorem frangant. Concilii Tridentini Acta*, 5:927. When priests are performing the rites of the Masses . . . let them also take care that they do not utter the words in so quiet a voice that they may not be easily understood by others, nor, on the other hand, in such fashion that they destroy the fervor of those who listen, by noise of a shouting voice [*clamoroso vocis strepitu*].

RODOLPHO HOSPINIANO

On the Origin of Organs in Churches (1603)

As a child, Rudolph Wirth (Rodolpho Hospinian, 1547–1626) saw his father arrested, imprisoned, and tortured for heresy. Likewise, his uncle was executed for heresy. Raised by a close family, Hospinian was educated in Zurich, and became a minister, academic, and author. He is among the first to tackle the organ question, basing much of his work on his father-in-law's, Ludwig Lavater (1527–1586).[1] No doubt fueled by

---

1. Compare, for example, this work of Lavater's with Hospianian: *Quo nunc ad Organa (ut vocant) attinet, constat eorum vsum veteri & Apostolicae ecclesiae prorsus incognitum, seroque inuentum atque receptum fuisse. Marianus Scotus in suis Chronicis, sub anno Domini 757. Organum, inquit, primum venisse in Franciam, missum Pipino regi à Constantino imperatore ex Graecia. Id quod Ioannes Auentinus annalium Boiorum lib. 3. fuius exponens scribit: Constantinus ad Pipinum iubet proficisci legatos. Munera quae à legatis deferebantur erant instrumentum musicae maximum, res adhuc Germanis & Gallis incognita, organum appellant, cicutis ex albo plumbo compactum est, simul & follibus inflatur & manuum pedumque digitis pulsatur, &c. Baleus Angliae episcopus, Vitellinaus ait patria Signinus vel Campanus, insignis musicus cantum in templis ordinauit (anno circiter Domini 660.) & organa per consonantias humanis vocibus adhibuit, iuxta illud Baptistae Mantuani: Signius adiunxit molli conflata metallo Organa, quae festis resonant ad sacra diebus. Haec organa aduersantur doctrinae Apostolicae I. Corinth. 14. De hoc iam nihil dicam quòd turpia & obscoena saepe cantantur, vt carnis potius voluptati quàm aedificationi spiritus seruiant. Lactantius Instit. lib. 2. cap. 7. acriter gentes taxat, quae Dei cultum constituerunt in ijs quae stultitia hominum admiratur. Adeóne inquit deorum religio nihil aliud est, quàm quod cupiditas humana miratur. Veniunt ad templa non tam religionis gratia, quàm vt videant & audiant quod oblectet, &c. Eras. quoque Roterodamus in I. ad Corinth. 14. doctè & grauiter contra vsum organorum in templis Christianorum disseruit. Praestaret igitur multorum doctrina & pietate celebrium virorum iudicio illa auferri ex templis. Quid enim nisi sonus inanis auditur sine verbis significantibus? Qui verò pridem haec ex templis sublata, non sine magna offensione restituunt, meritò sunt reprehendi. Videmus autem ferè accidere, vt in huiusmodi rebus reuocandis diligentes, in conseruanda*

his experience with the Roman Catholic Church, Hospinian's intent was to show that the Reformed had no use for the pipe organ: it had pagan origins, an abuse of the Roman Catholic Church, and a vestige of Old Testament (i.e. Judaical) worship.

Rodolpho Hospiniano, *De templis: hoc est, De origine, progressu, vsu et abusu templorum, ac omnino rerum omnium ad templa pertinentium.* Tiguri : Vvolfiana, 1603, V:XXIII:309-11:

On the origin of organs in churches, which the Germans call orgeln

At this time I will not speak of the origin or the inventors of the organs, or any other musical instruments, for that has already been done most excellently by Polydorus Vergilius *Of the Inventors of Things*, volume 1, chapter 15,[2] but only about that instrument which was added in the churches of the Christians to the religious singing, so that the harmony with the singing would be all the more pleasing and lovely, and which is called the *organ* in German.

Polydore Vergile in volume 1, chapter 15, states that *the name of the inventor of this our unsightly organ is not known*. David the great prophet of the Lord has indeed invented several musical instruments as is stated by Josephus *Antiquities of the Jews*, volume 7: "*And making a number of instruments he taught that the Levites would sing hymns of praise on them on the Sabbath days and on other festive days.*"[3] But the types of instruments

---

puritate doctrinae remissi sint & desides. Qui de musica in templis plura legere desiderat, consulat P. Martyrem in 14. cap. prioris epistolae ad Corinth. & 5. cap. lib. Iudicum: item Henr: Bulling. Decades in sermone de oratione. Lavertus, In libros paralipomenon, 60.

2. = Polydorus Vergilius (1470–1555), *De Rerum Inventoribus*, 1:15: *Nablum vero duodecim sonos habens, digitis tangitur, &c. Unde perspicere licet, istiusmodi Organa a Davide confecta diversissima fuisse a nostris, quorum nunc est usus in templis frequentissimus: illa enim plectro pulsabantur, nostra vero inflaktur follibus: unde multis meatibus cicutis imparibus quasi vox erumpit, concentuma efficit.*

3. = Flavius Josephus (34–100), *Flavii Iosephi Antiqvitatvm Ivdaicarvm*, VII:191ff: *Caeterum Dauid perfunctus iam bellis ac periculis, & in altissima pace degens, uario genere carminum odas & hymnos in honorem dei composuit, partim trimetro uerso, partim pentametro: instrumentisque musicis comparatis docuit Leuitas ad pulsum eorum laudes die decantare, tam sabbatis diebus, quàm in caeteris festiuitatibus. species autem instrumentorum hae fuere: cinnyra decem chordis intenditur, & plectro pulsatur: nabla duodecim sonos continet, sed digitis carpitur: cumque his aderant & cymbala aerea, bene magna atque lata: quo sanè de praedictorum instrumentorum natura, ne prorsus ignorentur, dixisse sufficit.*

of David were like this: A great sounding Cither with ten strings on it, and these were struck with a bat.

The Nablum instrument, which had twelve tones, was played by hitting with the fingers, etc. By which it becomes clear that the instruments that David created were very different from ours, which are now commonly used in the sanctuaries, for those were struck with a bat and ours are fed by wind from the bellows, which is fed through a number of conduits into different pipes which speak with a voice, and which make a harmony of song, as Polydore states in volume 1, chapter 15.

And the author of the *Responses to the Orthodox* which are appended to Justin [Martyr] indicates in the answer to question 107 that *in his days the custom in the church had been changed, that is from the Old Testament, to sing with lifeless instruments, and that the simple hymns had been kept as it appeared that the hymns with rattles and instruments pleased the children more than the congregation.* Without a doubt, they did that after the example of that age in which the Apostles were still alive, when they, as we read, sung poorly, without there being any mention of organs or other musical instruments.

Marinus Scotus describes in his chronicles that *around the year of our Lord 757 the organ first appeared in France, it having been sent to King Pepin by the Emperor Constantine of Greece*.[4] Aventinus's *History of the Dukes of Bavaria*, volume 3, page 300, further explains: *"Constantine ordered his emissaries to travel to Pippin; the gifts which were to be carried by the ambassadors were a very large musical instrument, an item which was still unknown to the Germans and Walloons. They called it an organ; it was built of white lead pipes, and it was powered by bellows and at the same time played with the hands and feet, etc."*[5] We can observe the same thing in *Annals of the Kings of the Franks, Pippin, Charlemagne & Louis* volume 4, chapters 64 and 113.[6]

---

4. = Mariani Scoti (1028–1083), *Chronica ad Euangelij ueritatem*, 396: 757 | 17 | *Organum primitus eunit in Francíam, missum Pipino Regi, à Constantino imperatore, de Graecia.*

5. = Johannes Aventinus (Johann Georg Turmair, 1477–1534), *Annales ducum Boiariae*, 404:17–23: *Constantinus ad Pipinum proficisci iubet legatos, quorum princeps Stephanus episcopus romanus. ipsi maritimo itinere cum muneribus ad Pipinum devenere. munera imperatoris, quae a legatis deferebantur, erant instrumentum musicae maximum, res aduc Germanis et Gallis incognita; organon adpellant. cicutis ex albo plumbo conpactum est, simul et follibus inflatur et manuum pedumque digitis pulsatur.*

6. = Hilduin Einhardus (775–840), *Annales Regum Francorum*, DCCLVII: *Misit Constantinus imperator regi Pippino cum aliis donis organum, qui in Franciam usque pervenit. Et rex Pippinus tenuit placitum suum in Compendio cum Francis; ibique Tassilo venit, dux Baioariorum, in vasatico se commendans per manus, sacramenta iuravit multa et*

1 | PROFESSORS

Baleus, a bishop in England states, *Vitellianus*,[7] *born in Sygnia or Campania, an outstanding musician, joined the singing in the churches and the organs to a harmony with the human voices*. As Mantuanus[8] writes in the fourth volume of Fastorum:

> [Pope Vitellianus who had been born in] Signia
> Wanted that there should be organs in the churches
> So that the people could hear them on festive days
> When the worship services were celebrated by all people.[9]

We read the same thing in Papal Chronicles,[10] and in Albrech Krantz's *Metropolis*, volume 2, chapter 1.[11]

In France these musical organs were first made around the year 828 at Aix through the ingenuity of a George from Venice,[12] a priest, at the

---

innumerabilia, reliquias sanctorum manus inponens, et fidelitatem promisit regi Pippino et supradictis filiis eius, domno Carolo et Carlomanno, sicut vassus recta mente et firma devotione per iustitiam, sicut vassus dominos suos esse deberet. Sic confirmavit supradictus Tassilo supra corpus sancti Dionisii, Rustici et Eleutherii necnon et sancti Germani seu sancti Martini, ut omnibus diebus vitae eius sic conservaret, sicut sacramentis promiserat; sic et eius homines maiores natu, qui erant cum eo, firmaverunt, sicut dictum est, in locis superius nominatis quam et in aliis multis.

7. = Pope Vitalian (?–672).

8. = Baptista Spagnuoli Mantuanus (F. Baptistae Mantvani, 1447–1516). But the quotation is misattributed to Mantuanus. Von Forkel, in *Allgemeine Geschichte*, 356ff, offers a source-critical history of the corrupted quote.

9. = John Bale (1495–1563), *Acta romanorum Pontificum*, 69: *Vitellianus, patria Signinus uel Campanus, musicus insignis, Ecclesiasticam regulam scripsit, cantum in templis ordinaiuit, & organa per consonantias humanis uocibus adhibuit: iuxta illud Baptistæ Mantuani, in quarto Fastorum libro: Signius adiunxit, molli conflata metallo | Organa, quæ festis resonant ad sacra diebus.*

10. Bartholomaeus Plantina (1421–1481), 76: *At Vitalianus cultui diuino intentus, & regulam ecclesiasticam composuit, & cantum ordinauit, adhibitis consonantiam (ut quidam uolunt) organis.*

11. = Albrecht Krantz (1450–1517), *Metropolis sive historia ecclesiastica Saxoniae*, 93: *VITALIANUS, patria signinus, oppido Volscorũ Papa creatur. Hic regulam clericorum composuit. Cantum per ecclesias ordinauit, adhibitis consonantium organis. Oratores in Angliam mittie, qui sluctuantes in fide Christi confirmarent. Anno sui pontificate 14. mense 6. moritur: ad concentum, ut consiiditur, euocatus angelorum.*

12. = Georgius, a Venetian priest, traditionally known as the first organ builder in the Western world after the fall of Rome. Emperor Louis the Pious commissioned Georgius to build an organ at Aix-la-Chapelle, his court, in the year 826. Georgius's pipe organ was a source of great prestige for the Frankish court, as documented in laudatory poems by Ermold le Noir and Walahfrid Strabo.

expense of King Louis as Aimonius recites in *Deeds of the Franks* Book 4, Chapter 114, with which Adventinus also agrees in volume 4.

In the course of time they went overboard in the construction of such organs, and no expense was spared to do so. Michael, the Emperor of Constantinople, had them made of gold, as Zonaras confirms in his third volume of *Histories*.[13] And Bruschius says in *The Monasteries of Germany*, page 107, that *George the Abbot of Salem had an organ built in the auditorium of his monastery, whose largest and central pipe was 28 feet long, and four spans in circumference*.[14]

How organs became more prominent around the year 1480 is described by Sabellicus in *Enneades*, volume 10, chapter 8 where he states: "*During the time of Pope Sixtus IV there was for a long time a man in Venice employed in the building of organs which nobody denies was the most excellent that there has ever been, by the name of Bernhardus, nicknamed the Teuton, in reference to the nation in which he had was born. He was the first to increase the number of registers on the organ, so that the feet also assisted in the music by pulling the cords.*"[15]

From this we gather that the use of this type of organ was totally unknown to the old and Apostolic churches, and was only later invented and accepted. Cardinal Thomas Cajetan also acknowledges this in his *Summula* in which he also states that the *Roman Catholic Church, as a symbol of this*,

---

13. = Johannes Zonaras (1070–1140), *Ioannis Zonarae Monachi*, 127: *Michael verò rerum potitus, tantas copias brevi tempore dilapidauit, in Mimos, adulatores, & aurigas insumptas, cum quidem eas totis plaustris, ut aiunt, effunderent. Thesauris iam exhaustis, quum tempus instaret pecuniae ijs distribuendae, qui dignitatibus praediti sunt, neque haberet unde largiretur: auream platanum, duos leones, totidem que gryphes, & organa, ex auro facta omnia, quae & Regiam ornabant, & exteris gentibus admirationi erant, conflauit, atque inde numismata cudi iussit.* While Zonaras names Michael III as commissioning the golden instrument, some research suggests that it was his father, Theophilos of Byzantium, who ordered the construction. The organ was then decorated with other treasures by Michael III. See Schuberth, *Kaiserliche Liturgie*, 75–77.

14. = Kaspar Brusch (1518–1557), *Monasteriorum Germaniae*, 107: *Georgius Monachus de Cõstantia, eligitaur in Abbatem Salemitanum anno 1441. Felice quinto pontificantui, Friderico terio Imperior, Henrico Barone de Heuuen Episcopatuipræsidente: præsuit annis pene 19. Resignauit Abbatiam anno 1459. Fecit fieri mius Organon, cuius maxima & medioxima Fistula habet in lõngitudine pedes 28, in circumferentia spithamas quatuor.*

15. = Marcus Antonius Coccius Sabellicus (1436–1506), *Rapsodiae historiarum Enneadum*, 328: *Venetiae habuerunt, Bernardum cognomento Theutonem, argumento gentis in qua ortus esset, omnia musicae artis instrumenta scientissime tractauit, primus in Organis auxit numeros, vt & pedes quoque iuuarent concentum funiculone attractu, mira in eo artis eruditio, voxque ad omnes numeros accomodata, numinis puidentia ad it natus, ut unus esset in quo ars pulcherrima omnes vires experiret suas.*

1 | PROFESSORS

does not use any organ in the presence of the Pope even in these days; just the same he adds that the use of them is permitted for the sake of the human and imperfect believers.

But it is in conflict with the teachings of the apostles in 1 Corinthians 14. I will not speak of it at this time, that often scandalous and dishonest matters are expressed with the sound of the organ in such a way that they serve more to the sensuality of the flesh than to the edification of the congregation. Lactanius in his *Institutes*, volume 2, chapter 7 severely chastises the heathens that encompassed the service of God in those things, about which the insanity of the people wonder, stating: "*Is the service of God no more than what the people desire?*"[16] They come to church not so much because of their religion, but in order to see and hear those things that delight them.

And could we not say this about all Christians as well? At times I have seen many leave the church in astonishment and also a few when the sweet sounds of the organ stopped. That is the kind of devotion that it had aroused in the hearts of the people. Which is the reason why Erasmus[17] in *Annotations* on 1 Corinthians 14 argued scholarly and effectively against the use of the organs in churches, and he stated not unreasonably: "*Not content with these things, we have brought into the sanctuaries some kind of elaborate and theatrical music, a noisy twittering of varied voices, such as I do not believe was ever heard in Greek or Roman theaters. Trumpets, crumhorns, shawms, and sackbuts resound everywhere competing with the voices of the people. Sexual and filthy ditties are heard, the kind to which whores and buffoons dance. One flocks together in church as if it were a theater to delight their ears. To this end, organists are supported with high salaries, and crowds of children, whose entire youth is wasted in arduously learning such*

---

16. = Lucius Coelius Firmianus Lactantius (250–317), L[ucii] Coelii Lactantii Firmiani Divinarum institutionum, 65: . . . an ideo religio Deorum nihil aliud est, quod cupiditas humana miratur?

17. = Desiderius Erasmus (1466–1536), *In novum Testamentum annotationes*, 508: Nec his contenti operosam quandam ac theatricam musicam, in sacras aedes induximus, tumultuosum diuersarum vocum garritum, qualem non opinor in Graecorum aut Romanorum theatris unquam auditorum fuisse. Omnia tubis, lituis, fistulis, ac sambucis perstrepunt: cumque his certant hominum voces. Audiuntur amatoriae foedaeque cantilenae, ad quas scorta mimique saltitant. In sacram aedem velut in theatrum concurritur, ad delinendas aures. Et in hunc usum magnis salariis aluntur organorum opifices, puerorum greges, quorum omnis aetas in perdiscendis huiusmodi gannitibus consumitur: nihil interim bonae rei discentium. Alitur sordidorum, ac levium, ut plerique sunt Dionysiaci, hominum colluvies, ac tantis sumptibus oneratur ecclesia ob rem pestiferam etiam. Quaeso te ut rationem ineas, quot pauperes de vita periclitantes, poterant ali cantorum salariis? . . . . Cur haec nobis sola placent, quae Paulus ceu parvulorum infantiam parcissime vult adhiberi, imò quae nullo pacto laturus fuerat?

warblings, meanwhile studying nothing of substance. The vulgar and frivolous are salaried, as many of them are Dionysiacs,[18] *the sewage of humanity, and the Church is also burdened with so many expenses due to this noxious affair. I ask you, can you calculate how many poor folk, dying in want, could be supported with the stipends of singers? . . . . How is it that only these things please us, that Paul was willing to be used only sparingly with the immaturity of children, no, rather which will by no means be tolerated?"*

Again, Erasmus writes about this in *Lingua* page 68: *"But what is more elaborate than present-day music, mimicking the chatter of many birds with such a large number of vocal parts? What would the Spartan magistrate Emerepes say now? He was the man who cut off two strings of the musician Phyrnis's nine-stringed lyre with a two-edged ax, saying* Don't ruin the music. *Supposing he heard one and the same organ being played in the houses of God imitating trumpets, horns, bugles, recorders, tenor, alto, thunder, and the voices of men and birds? The standard of our music reflects that of our fashion in clothing and furnishings and architecture. The original simplicity is nowhere, and elaborate caprices grow daily more common."*[19]

This is the reason why it is a good thing, according to the opinion of those men who are renowned for their scholarship and piety, that these organs should be removed from the sanctuaries. For let us not [use] those objects in our worship service, which were provided in the Old Testament by musical instruments. For in the first place, those instruments (as we have said above) are different from the ones we use. Secondly, Procopius of Gaza[20] writes in his [biblical] commentary on the book of Kings, chapter 4, that this type of worship has not been ordained by God but was initiated by David. In the third place, the Lord has allowed many things to happen with his former people which he no longer wants to see those who have become complete men through Christ burdened with.

18. Erasmus's label for professional singers.

19. Desiderius Erasmus, *Lingua sive de linguae*, 4:673: *Quid autem hodie operosius nostra musica, tot vocibus multarum avium garritum imitans? Quid diceret Emerepes ille Laconum Ephorus, qui Phrynidis musici duas e nouem chordas incidit bipenni dicens* ne corrumpas musicam [Μή κακούργει τήν μουσικήν], *si nunc audiret in templis eadem organa referre, tubas cornua lituos tibias apertas, tibias obscuriores, tibias raucas, tonitrua, voces hominum et volucrum? Qualis est musica nostra, talis est cultus, talis victus, talis aedificatio. Prisca simplicitas nusquam est, indies augescunt operosae deliciae.*

20. = Procopius of Gaza (465–529), *Commentarii in octateuchum*, 538: *Hic sigitu docuit propheta, quod spiritus deceptionis, qui impiis hominibus pro organis & instrumentis utitur, mendaciter uictoriam promittat. Hoc autem sit Deo permittente. Cum enim prohibere potuisset, non prohib uit.*

ANDRÉ RIVET

Prologomena to the Psalms (excerpt, 1626)

As a French Hugenot, Andreas Rivetus (1572–1651) would not have known the use of the organ in services of worship. Over the course of his lifetime, his anti-orgel stance did not waver despite acquaintance with Dutch royals and a visit to England.

Commentarius in Psalmorum propheticorum de mysteriis evangelicis dodecadem selectam. Lugduni Batavorum: I. & J. Commelini, 1626, 3ff:

The ecclesiastical and ordinary use of musical instruments, by royal command, was introduced under David following the counsel of the prophets Gad and Nathan. Under Hezekiah it was restored. II Chronicles 29:25 says, "*The Levites sang in the house of the Lord, with cymbals and psaltery, and harps, in the way prescribed by David the king, and of Gad the seer, and of Nathan the prophet.*" And this was not a human institution, for it adds, "*this was commanded by the Lord through his prophets.*" Therefore Procopius of Gaza is false in this matter, who in his *Commentary on the First Book of Kings* says, "*It is easy to see that this worship was not handed down from God but from David,* παρὰ θεοῦ μὲν οὐ δέδιται," he says. Chrysostom[1] on Psalm 150 says that those instruments were permitted to the Israelites on account of their weakness.[2] The author of the questions attributed to Justin Martyr gives the same reason in Question 107, where he says, "*Since songs*

1. = John Chrysostom (344–407).
2. *imbecillitatem.*

were composed by unbelievers for the sake of deception, they were enjoined to those under the law because of the childishness of their minds. Why should those who have received the perfect Law of Grace, and contrary to the ways of those just mentioned, use songs in their churches in the manner of children under the law? Answer: Plain singing is not childish, but only the singing with lifeless organs, with dancing and castanets, etc. Then, in the church, the use of such instruments, and other things fit for children, is taken away from the songs, and singing alone remains. Musical instruments of this sort move the mind toward pleasure, rather than forming some good state of mind, drawn toward devotion and for the formation of good character, etc." From which it is agreed that at the time of Justin the use of organs was not introduced into the churches. Bellarmine, *On Good Works* in particular I.17[3] confesses that this usage is not suitable for the perfect, and that it began to be admitted in the church lately, certainly around the time of Pope Vitalian around AD 650, from the calculation of Platinas. If we believe Haymo the monk, book 4 *On the Deeds of the Franks*, chapter 114,[4] before the time of Louis the Pius, that is in the year 840, organ music had not been heard in the churches except in the Western church. It was a certain Greek minister, George by name, whom Baldric the count and prefect of Pannonia had introduced to the emperor, who was the first author who urged the emperor to receive music of this sort, *previously unused in the kingdom of the Franks*. Nevertheless, what had been accepted by the emperor, perhaps for private use, was not afterwards adopted everywhere at that time. For Thomas Aquinas, who flourished long after the time of Louis the Pius, certainly around the year 1270, in the second part of the second question, 91, Art. 2, testifies about the church of his time, that organ music had not been received into it. "The church," he says, "*does not take up musical instruments like harps and psaltery in divine praises lest it appear to imitate the Jews*." He adds that in the Old Testament there was the use of such instruments because the people at that time were both harder and more carnal, who had to be provoked through such instruments, and as well because physical instruments of this sort prefigured something spiritual. Cajetan and George of Venice, weighing Thomas's words carefully, recognize that at the

---

3. = Roberto Francesco Romolo Bellarmine (1542–1621), *De Bonis Operibus*: It is Part 3 of controversy 15 in Bellarmine's massive treatise, *Disputationes de controversiis*.

4. = Floriacensis Aimonus (965–1008), *Historiae Francorum*, 4:64:408: *Historiae Francorum libri quinque Constantinus imperator misit Pipino regi multa munera, inter quae & organum, quae ad eum Compendium perlata sunt: ubi tunc populi sui generalem conventum habuit.*

time of Thomas there was no use of organs in the church. Thomas adds deeply philosophical reasons why it would not be fitting for this to be so. He says that Aristotle taught in book 8 of the *Politics* that flutes should not be employed in teaching, nor any other artificial musical instrument, i.e. a lyre, and any other such that exists. But only what makes the hearers better. For musical instruments of this sort move the soul more toward delight than the good interior disposition formed through it. Thus far Aristotle. Whence Cajetanus infers that musical instruments must not be admitted into church services, in which we gather for the sake of taking up divine interior discipline, and that they must all the more be excluded as the divine interior discipline is more excellent than all human disciplines, since they repel instruments of this sort.

This restriction of Cajetan seems consistent with reason, that the use of musical instruments not be admitted into church services. Otherwise, apart from church services, we consider the use of organs a matter of indifference, although I would prefer that it [the use of organs] be completely removed from the churches, lest *certain people come to the churches not so much for the sake of religion as that they may see or hear something,* by which Lactantius takes to task the peoples in *Institutes* 2.7. And Erasmus, the great ornament of the Netherlands in his *Commentary* on 1 Corinthians 14, complains that a certain overwrought and theatrical music has been brought into the churches the likes of which he thought unheard before in the theaters of the Greeks and Romans, and that all the horns, curved trumpets, flutes, and shrill-stringed instruments made excessive noise. But more of these things later, perhaps more than enough.

GISBERTUS VOETIUS

Letter to Constantijn Huygens (1641)

This letter is between two leading figures of the Dutch organ controversy. Constantijn Huygens just published his book Orgel Gebruyckt *in 1641 and sent Voetius a presentation copy. Voetius, who will disagree with Huygens's conclusions, writes this adroit letter which simply acknowledges the reception of the book without necessarily endorsing its conclusions. Voetius's "detailed, future publication" is his essay that follows.*

A. C. Duker, *Gisbertus Voetius*. Leiden: Brill, 1910, 125:

Letter of Gisbertus Voetius to Constantijn Huygens, March, 1641

Utrecht, 8 March, 1641.

Most noble and magnificent sir,

I have received two copies of your dissertation on the use and abuse of the organ, one of which I have passed on to our heroic lady Schurman.[1] She gives thanks for the literary gift, as do I, most profoundly. Indeed I would have liked to write my opinion out now in full, if certain other works in preparation, whose publication now is pressing, did not hinder me. And I

---

1. The reference to the "heroic lady Schurman" is to Anna Maria van Schurman, the only female student allowed to matriculate at Utrecht at that time; importantly, with the assistance and blessing of Voetius. Though Anna Maria could attend class, she could only do so from sitting in a niche, behind a curtain. See Irwin, ed., *Anna Marie van Schurman*.

would reserve this entire matter, whatever it is, for a more precise discussion to be published some other time. I here display the image of our Schurman, which she herself painted and engraved, if perhaps you have not yet seen it, together with some verses with which she tried in vain to persuade the distinguished jurist Schotanus[2] to delay his departure. I pray that God will govern you with his Spirit, in order that you may continue (to the best of your abilities in such an unsuitable place and age) to further grace and advance with your extraordinary and admirable example the study of true wisdom and godliness.

The most obedient servant of your nobility and magnificence,
Gisbertus Voetius

---

2. = Christian Schotanus (1603–1672), a professor of Greek at the Academy of Franecker.

IONNES HEIMENBERGIUS AND GISBERTUS VOETIUS

The Organ and Organ Music, part 1 (1641, 1661)

A champion of unadorned congregational singing is the illustrious professor Gisbertus Voetius. Teaching in his position at Utrecht's then newly founded university, Voetius was the leading opponent of the pipe organ (anti-orgelist) not only in Utrecht, but also for the entire Dutch Republic of the time. Voetius wrote on the subject of proper worship in general, and the use of the pipe organ in particular, no less than four times, and even included a ninety-six-page essay on the subject in his magnum opus, Politicæ ecclesiasticæ.[1] *The anti-orgelist essay translated here is invaluable for its scope and bibliographical references as well as its theological architecture that built the anti-orgelist position after Calvin's death, giving insight into the mind of second-generation Reformers such as Dr. Voet. In addition, Voetius's influence extended far beyond Utrecht once the city's young university began graduating Reformed ministers who served churches across the Dutch republic.*

Johannes Heimenbergius's dissertation on the use and misuse of the pipe organ was researched under the supervision of his mentor, Gisbertus Voetius. As was common in the academy of that day, it was Heimenbergius's thesis that was published under Voetius's name in Politicæ Ecclesiasticæ *with his edits (indicated in the following text). Both extant works are archived together in the Koninklijke Bibliotheek, The Hague: Hs KA XLVIII.*

---

1. Gisbertus Voetius, *Politicæ ecclesiasticæ*, 4 vols. (Amsterdam: Joannis a Wæsberge, 1663–1676), 2:III. Hereafter *PE*.

1 | PROFESSORS

When Voetius became a professor of theology and oriental languages at Utrecht's new gymnasium illustre *on Monday, August 21, 1634—inexplicably, just one day after preaching his farewell sermon in Heusden on August 20, 1634, Prof. Voet worked tirelessly to promote the gymnasium to a full university in about two years' time. In addition to his full teaching schedule, Voetius gave no less than eight public lectures in his first year alone. Then, on September 13, 1634, Voetius complemented this work with the introduction of Saturday disputations. These were semi-private seminars where students, colleagues, and local pastors could debate openly church polity, ethics, praxis, and theology. They took the following form: Voetius composed a thesis touching on the pressing issues of the day. Appointed defenders were then instructed on how to debate and defend the thesis. Other attendees would challenge the debaters. Final redactions of these debates form the heart of* Politicæ Ecclesiasticæ, *including the role of the pipe organ and organ music that was one of the first topics of these disputations.*

However, and importantly, David van Boxtel (1614–1666), an attendee at the disputations, did not judge Voetius's teaching to be sound, nor did van Boxtel's colleague Jacobus Johannes Batelier (1593–1672), a minister living in The Hague. In only a matter of weeks, Batelier published a response in which he said of Voetius's teaching as a whole: "If I should enumerate the empty inquiries put forward by Voetius, I would wholeheartedly say that it will be necessary to rethink the major part of the list of his arguments."[2] *Voetius countered these attacks in a comprehensive work, addressed to "a certain anonymous dweller in darkness,"[3] entitled* Thersites the Self-Tormentor. That is, The Remonstrants' Champion Subdued, after Insulting once again the German, French, and Dutch Catechism and Liturgy; and the Same Challenged to Prove the Lies and Accusations which He Poured Out upon the Appointed Lords and Most Noble Magistrates of the Dutch Republic, the Reformed Religion, the Churches, the Synods, the Pastors, etc, without Reason or Moderation.[4] *Though he argues with his opponents on other major theological issues of the day, Voetius*

---

2. Jacob Johannes Batelier, *Examen accuratum disputationis*, 60. Batelier was deposed in 1619 as a remonstrant.

3. *L. tenebrio.*

4. *Thersites Heautontimorumenos.* θερσίτης is an Homeric name meaning "the audacious." Εαυτόν τιμωρούμευος is the title of a play by Menander, the "self-tormentor."

does mention the organ question ever so briefly on pages 293–94, and reprints them later in his Appendix Apologetica *(which follows here).*

Thersites *may have silenced adversaries for a time, but in 1649 another assault came from Samuel Maresius (1599–1673)[5] who also refuted Voetian theology, including a challenge to Voetius's anti-organ stance.[6]*

After these two published attacks, twenty-seven years after the first disputations, Voetius published his Church Polity (Politicae Ecclesiasticae), *the massive four-volume work that reviews everything from church organization and ecclesiastical law, to the daily life of a minister and, to our point, the use of the pipe organ in worship. As mentioned above, Voetius reprinted Heimenbergius's thesis under his name after altering with his own corrections, additions, and redactions. Voetius followed this entry with his own* Appendix Apologetica. *As the title suggests, this* Appendix *is a brief essay that summarizes Voetius's stance on the organ in general while serving as a counter-attack against Batelier's and Maresius's published works in specific. Interestingly, Voetius does clarify here that his earlier writing against the organ had to do with solo organ music; apparently, only after the 1634 disputation did he become aware that some churches were using the organ to accompany their psalmody.[7]*

---

5. = Samuel Desmarets (1599–1673), *Theologus paradoxus retectus et refutatus.* The full title is so colorful it deserves translation: *A bizarre theologian unmasked and refuted, or some academic exercises of Samuel Maresius opposed to the twelve paradoxes, and the unreasonably toxic disputations, openly held against him in the lyceum of Utrecht, by Gisbertus Voetius, the ranking theologian in that place; whose one hundred slippery, dangerous and altogether bizarre propositions are faithfully recounted and refuted.*

6. *Musica organica nec pars est nec appendix cultus divini. Ita habet in Disp. inaug. Coroll. Eccle. 8. & in Thersite sect. 3. cap. 3. Absurde: Quamvis enim nec pars sit essentialis, nec appendix necessaria & ad esse cultus divini, tamen pro appendice debet haberi, ad melius & commodius esse, ubicunque, ut speciatim in hac Ecclesia, inter ipsum cultum usurpatur, ex generali praecepto Pauli I Cor XIV, 48. quo praeveniantur incommodo ipsum interturbatura, qualis esset dissonantia canentium. Neque debet hic homo metuere ne Organista ea ratione consistuatur Minister Ecclesiasticus. Licet enim non censeatur Minister ex eo genere Ministerii quod Christus ad esse instituit, & quale exercent Pastores, Seniores, Diaconi, erit tamen ex eo genere Ministrorum quos Ecclesia ad bene esse instituit, cujusmodi sunt Canicidae, Ostiarii, & Praecentores.* Maresius, 226–27.

7. *Anno 1634. cum Disputationem illam proponerem, & defensionem ejus contra Remonstrant-Socinianum Aggressorem conscriberem, cujus editio sequenti anno demum absolvebatur, ne per somnium quidem cogitabam nec fando unquam audiveram de cantu Organi cum cantu Psalmorum, nec ullibi in Ecclesiis Belgicis talis cantus exstabat; quippe*

1 | PROFESSORS

What follows now are excerpts of Voetius's writing on the organ. First, the Heimenbergius thesis of 1641, published later with Voetius's edits in 1663. Then a sampling from the Appendix Apologetica, *the first and last paragraphs. Together, these works display for us Voetius's foundation of his anti-orgelist stance, the level of vitriol that the organ controversy elicited, and that over time Voetius's opinion on organ use did not waver.*

Abbreviated Timeline

August 1634: Voetius becomes professor in Utrecht
September 1634: Saturday disputations begin
1634: Batelier and van Boxtel publish against Voetius
1635: Voetius publishes against Batelier and van Boxtel
1637: Synod of Delft allows each congregation to decide organ question
1641: Huygens publishes pro-organ book *Orgel Gebruykt*
1641: Voetius writes to Huygens, promising a "detailed future" publication on organ use
1641: Heimenbergius finishes his anti-organ thesis with Voetius
1649: Maresius publishes against Voetius
1663: Volume one of Voetius's *Church Polity* is published, included is Heimenbergius's altered thesis followed by *Appendix Apologetica*.

Ionnes Heimenbergius, *De organis et canu organico in Sacro [sub præsidio Gisberti Voetii]*

Ultraiecti: Ægidii Roman, 1641.
　The First Part of
　A Theological Disputation
　Of Ecclesiastical Polity
　CONCERNING

---

primum in Ecclesiâ aliquâ Hollandicâ N. Aedilis alicujus aut Aedilium istius loci privato judicio ac studio anno 1637. introductus. PE, 593. In the year 1634, when I had set forth that disputation and composed its defense against a Remonstrant-Socinian aggressor, whose publication eventually came out in the next year, even in my dreams I was not thinking, nor had I heard in any talking, about organ music together with psalm-singing. Nor did such music exist anywhere in the Dutch churches, because [it was] first introduced in the year 1637 in some church in [the province of] North Holland by the private judgment and eagerness of a magistrate or magistrates of that place.

Organs and Organ Music
In worship,
Which
With the help of God the Greatest and Best,
Under the guidance of
Master Gisbertus Voetius, Doctor of Sacred Theology,
and also Professor of the same Faculty in the Renowned Academy of Utrecht,
and p.t. [*pro tempore*] Rector Magnificus, and in the Church in that place
a most vigilant Pastor,

I,
Johannes Heimenbergius of Utrecht,
Will attempt to defend,
On the 3rd of July at the time and place customary.

UTRECHT:
From the workshop of Aegidius Roman, printer for the Academy,
in the year 1641.

To a man eminent because of the most ancient nobility of his family,
Master Johan van Reede[8]
Magistrate in Renswoude, etc., Delegate of the Province of Utrecht to the Assembly of the Most Powerful Lords by the name of the States–General,
he offers this disputation submissively, and with a thankful heart.
Johannes Heimenbergius. Respondent

---

8. = Johan van Reede van Renswouden (1593–1682), a Dutch diplomat and politician.

1 | PROFESSORS

[Voetius omits this introductory paragraph of Heimenbergius:]

The universal wellspring of nearly all corruptions in religion is showing off one's learning[9] and that insane wisdom of the flesh by which the simplicity of faith and the "foolishness"[10] of evangelical preaching is defiled. Hence the painting of words and the production of ceremonies and rites are usually sought out eagerly—to adorn simple piety more greatly, of course—but in fact to crush it with their own weight, unless they are suppressed. The ornamentation and embellished[11] noise of music[12] by voices and by instruments in church worship do part of this in a highly colored manner. Although we have discussed this several times before now in public lectures,[13] following the ordinance for common spaces, now we are compelled to set forth the totality of our ideas in this learned discourse; first so that we may so much the better lead our students, but also especially so that we might be of service to others, who demand this from us as some sort of duty. We have omitted many questions regarding music in church; thus, in the present treatise we treat only organ music. We will explain: I. The general controversy, which is open and commonly known. II. Controversies both more specific and more obscure. III. Certain cases and practical problems.

[Voetius adds: Chapter 3. Concerning Organs and organ music in worship

Concerning organ music, we are about to explain: I. the general controversy. II. more specific controversies. III. certain mistakes and more practical problems.]

---

9. δοκησισοφία.

10. μωρία. See 1 Corinthians 1:23: "ἡμεῖς δὲ κηρύσσομεν Χριστὸν ἐσταυρωμένον, Ἰουδαίοις μὲν σκάνδαλον ἔθνεσιν δὲ μωρίαν."

11. πολυποίκιος.

12. Joseph Dyer notes, "In the Middle Ages, the term *musica* applied properly to the speculative science that considered proportional relationships, while *cantilena* and *cantus* referred to sounding music." ("Place of *Musica*," 3n1) Thus, depending on context, the translation here translates *cantus* as *music, sound, musical performance*, or even *performance practice*.

13. Heimenbergius here references Voetius's famous Saturday afternoon seminars. The organ question was the first topic of the first disputations in August of 1634, the inaugural year of the *illustere school* of Utrecht—as Voetius himself will recall later in this chapter (though a participant, Martin Schoock, dates them not during August, but on July 3 and July 10, 1634. Schoock, *Exercitationes*, 516).

§1. In the chief controversy about to be explained in detail, there occur 1. Presuppositions. 2. Hypotheses, postulates, and givens.[14] 3. Status of the controversy. 4. Arguments. 5. Solutions to the objections. 1. Presupposition of the terms is 1. of those which pertain to the subject of the question: they are sound or music, organ,[15] organ music or organ sound. 1. Musical sound is modulated sound, as the natural philosophers[16] teach. It is divided into simple and complex sound, and the latter again into ornamented and harmonic sound.[17] Harmonic sound again variously is divided by mode, by material, and by medium: leaving other divisions to musicians, we pick only two by mode, and one by object or material, and finally one by cause or medium, because they touch upon this dispute of ours. As regards the mode of mensuration, one is simple, which they call equal-measured[18] and Gregorian; the other is "chromatic" or mensurally notated,[19] which they call Ambrosian.[20] Again as regards the modes of varying counterpoint and harmonic consonance, one is the motet, the other the madrigal.[21] As regards the material or object, one is holy or special and either in private use or in ecclesiastical use; the other common or profane. Of the source or medium, one is vocal, another instrumental, another mixed. 2. Organ, or instrument (by synecdoche, a musical [instrument], which the Hebrews call "to be able."[22] 2 Chronicles 4:22, Amos 6:5); in this type is every inanimate lifeless thing[23] (1 Corinthians 14:7) which apart from the human and animal

14. διδόμενα.

15. The 1663 edition adds a comma here that was not in the 1641 Aegidius Romanus printing.

16. *docent Physici*. After 1834, this profession would be coined "scientist."

17. *in Fractum, & in Harmonicum* as in 1641 Aegidius Romanus printing. The 1663 edition mistakenly printed *Tractum, & in Harmonicum*.

18. *choralem*.

19. *figuralis*.

20. Here Heimenbergius and Voetius borrow terms of rhythmic modes of notation from sixteenth-century German music theory. "Equal-measured" [*choralem*] does not mean "choral," but using notes of equal length. "Mensurally notated" [*figuralis*] refers to rhythmic notation using notes of varying lengths. "Chromatic" refers to notational practices of the late Renaissance rhythms rather than to mode or harmony. Finally, the references to "Gregorian" and "Ambrosian" are problematic: while their labels indicate a specific range and tonal system, there is no difference in their rhythms, the topic of the sentence.

21. *Moetticus* and *madrigalicus* are actually adjectives, but there is no equivalent in English.

22. בלי.

23. ἄψυχον.

voice is used for music or modulated sound. It is divided moreover into that which can be touched[24] (which they also call struck and strung[25]); and into wind[26] or breathing:[27] the former produces harmony in a single strike; the latter either by wind and touch together, or by wind alone. Scripture enters into this dichotomy of all instruments farther (1 Corinthians 14:7 and Genesis 4:21) where by synecdoche, from any category, one principal or very well-known form is indicated. The passage Daniel 3: 5, 7, 10 lays out the division fully through the same reasoning. The reasoning of the same [divisions] can be assumed also in Psalm 150: 3–5 and 1 Chronicles 25:1–5 and 2 Chronicles 5:12–13. The types of struck instruments[28] are usually divided into those which are struck on [metal] strings (as the psaltery, pandura,[29] clavichord, cithara); those which [are struck] on gut strings[30] (as tortoise-shell lyre,[31] harp, lyre, tympanum,[32] or small lyre[33]); those which [are struck] on bronze: (as the bell, cymbal, sistrum); or again, those which are touched either with fingers, or with a plectrum or mallet. The types of wind instruments[34] are usually divided into: *First*, those that are played by the action of wind or breathing; in water-organs where water [pressure] causes a breeze or air flow; in blown instruments, where human breath does this; in instruments pumped by bellows,[35] where bellows do this, and on places exposed to the sun[36] where the rays of the sun or the movement of the light does this. *Second*, those instruments that are classified by their form into the categories of fistula [reed pipe], tibia [flute], bucina [horn], tuba [trumpet], cornu

24. ψηλαφητόν.

25. κρουστόν & ἔντατον.

26. πνευματικόν.

27. ἐμπνευστον.

28. κρουσῶν.

29. The 1663 edition refers to a *panduta*, surely a typographical error that should have been *pandura*.

30. *nervis seu fidibus*.

31. Voetius gives both the Latin and Greek names, *testudo* and *chelys*, respectively.

32. A string instrument with a drum-shaped body and a neck, with strings running the entire length.

33. *fidicula*.

34. πνευματικῶν.

35. *follica*.

36. *solarium*. *Solarium* can denote a sunroom, any part of the house exposed to sun, a balcony, or even a sundial. Here I think Heimenbergius is referencing the wind experienced on a terrace.

[horn], utriculum [small bagpipe] etc.,[37] and that which unites all those things and more in itself, that machine which strictly and par excellence[38] they now call the organ; and now we must properly deal with its music. I leave questions of [its] material, form, parts, construction, and use, etc. to writers on building a music instrument or an organ: I am content to have warned, with three statements about its origin and antiquity, that it [the organ] cannot be derived from sacred writings, and therefore, that the increase either of its predominance or of its use in services cannot be derived from sacred writings. Genesis 4:21. Job 21:12; 30:31. Ezekiel 33:32. Psalm 150:4. For the Greek Septuagint explains עגב by "the harp and singing,"[39] but only Psalm 150:4 by "organ."[40] The Targum has everywhere *anubah*,[41] a reed pipe of the Jews. The Arabic translation of Genesis 4 switches tambourine and cithara. The *Arabic Paraphrase of the Psalms* published at Rome, as it translates the Greek text (if not the Latin Vulgate) more often than the Hebrew one, retains the word "organum" in Psalm 150. The Syrian paraphraser, as published by Erpenius,[42] has "strong instruments." Kimchi,[43] commenting on Psalm 150, says that it is a musical instrument unknown to us. And Aben Ezra[44] says on Genesis 4, concerning either instrument named there, nothing other than that it is a type of musical instrument, and so also Rabbi Solomon Jarchi[45] on Psalm 150. Furthermore, whatever the interpreters, commentators, and lexicographers may call it, it is certain that neither from the etymology of the voice nor from the circumstances of the texts is it possible to derive an instrument[46] strictly called thus. It is not improbable that at least some kind

---

37. The buccina, tuba, cornu, and utriculum were all instruments used for military signaling.

38. κάτ εξοχήν.

39. ψαλτήριον & ψαλμόν. The passage could be Psalm 80:2 [= Psalm 81:2], although the two words are not next to each other: "λάβετε ψαλμὸν καὶ δότε τύμπανον, ψαλτήριον τερπνὸν."

40. όργανον.

41. אנובא.

42. = Thomo Erpino (Thomas van Erpe, 1584–1624). The work is probably *Psalmi Davidis*.

43. = Rabbi David Kimchi (Kimhi, Qimchi, RaDaK, 1160–1235).

44. = Rabbi Aben Ezra (Abraham ben Meir ibn Ezra, 1092–?).

45. = Rabbi Solomon Jarchi (Rashi, 1040–1105).

46. *organum*.

1 | PROFESSORS

of wind instrument[47] is intended in the cited passages, Genesis 4 and Psalm 150; what type, however, of wind instrument it is, since the Holy Spirit does not teach us, in vain we exhaust ourselves to determine, with absurd and transitory conjectures. However, this does nothing for our inquiry into its origin or age from secular antiquity, since it very often depends upon uncertain and insubstantial conjectures. Because of the ambiguity of the word "organ," here many deceive themselves and others. The organ[48] with which we are dealing today strictly concerns that labor-intensive and extraordinary machine, even as the Hebrews and so also the ancient Greeks used the term about whatever musical instrument is either struck[49] or makes use of wind,[50] as can be seen in Pollux's *Onomasticon*, book 4, chapters 9 and 10.[51] Although the title [of chapter 10] is *The Kinds of Organs*[52] the text refers to nothing but a type of tibia [flute]. Thus Athenaeus[53] in book 4 calls the hydraulicon of Ctesibius a "water-organ."[54] On the contrary, after those or similar machines were introduced into Greece, and from that place carried over to the West, more recent Greeks have not stopped calling by this name either any such instrument in general, or reed pipe in particular: hence *organarios*,[55] player of the reed pipe,[56] in the Greco-Latin glosses, in Meursius, in *A Greek Barbarian Glossary*.[57] And Bartholomaeus Anglicus [Voetius adds: who flourished in the 1460[58] has made almost the same distinction in book 20 of *On the Properties of Things*, chapter 132.]

47. πνευματικόν.
48. οργανον.
49. κρουομένω.
50. πνευματικώ.
51. = Iulius Pollux (?-238), *Iulii Pollucis Onomasticon*.
52. εἴδη ὀργάνων.
53. Athenaeus lived in the third century. He writes (lib IV:174) that the hydraulis was invented in the time of the second Ptolemy Euergetes, by Ctesibius (Ktsibios or Κτησίβιος, 285–222 BC), a native of Alexandria and by profession a barber. Ctesibius improved the hydraulis. Plato would later reference the hydraulic organ and a "night clock" organ—its flute pipes played the hours of the night throughout the darkness.
54. ὀργανον ἰδραυλικόν.
55. ὀργανάριος.
56. *organarius, fistularius*.
57. = Ioannis Meurius (Johannes van Meurs, 1579-1639), *Glossarium, graeco-barbarum*. *Glossarium* was one of the first dictionaries of modern Greek, the "barbarian language."
58. *De proprietatibus rerum*. But Voetius's inserted date here is problematic. Bartholomaeus Angilcus did not flourish in 1460—he was a thirteenth-century mystic. This is certainly a typographical error, meant to be 1260.

In short, neither from Greek nor from the Romans has today's acceptance of this meaning come down, but from more recent Frenchmen who call this particular instrument *orgues*, as Henry Stephano notes in his *Thesaurus*.[59] Look therefore how skillfully our organ has been derived from Latin, Greek, and Hebrew antiquities, as often as the word "organ" occurs anywhere. I do not deny, however, the water reed pipes, wide-mouthed round jars[60] giving forth harmony, wind-jars, Tritons blowing trumpets,[61] and also those constructions by Ctesibius and other artisans, played by the impact of water. However, these others are different from our organs, as from their description it is collected in the writings of Vitruvius book 9 chapter 9, Athenaeus book 4 and 11, and Polydore Vergil turns his attention to this well in *Concerning Inventors*,[62] book 1, chapter 14 and book 3, chapter 7. And Jules-César Boulenger,[63] *Concerning Theater*, book 2, chapter 32. Dalecampius[64] on Pliny book 7 chapter 37 in which see more annotations from antiquity. Salmasius also gathers several things in his *Exercitationes ad Solinum*[65] chapter 37[66] page 638. And these things are already known with respect to the subject, concerning sound and concerning the organ; whence automatically a description and division of sound or organ music follows.

59. = Henrico Stephano (Henri Estienne, 1528/31–1598), *Thesaurus Graecae linguae*.

60. πίθη πνευστικά.

61. Literally, *conch-shells*.

62. *De inventoribus rerum*, 1:15: "Nablum vero duodecim sonos habens, digitis tangitur, &c. Unde perspicere licet, istiusmodi Organa a Davide confecta diversissima fuisse a nostris, quorum nunc est usus in templis frequentissimus: illa enim plectro pulsabantur, nostra vero inflaktur follibus: unde multis meatibus cicutis imparibus quasi vox erumpit, concentuma efficit." The Nablum instrument, which had twelve tones, was played by hitting with the fingers, etc. by which it becomes clear that the instruments that David created were very different from ours, which are now commonly used in the sanctuaries, for these were struck with a bat and ours are fed by wind from the bellows, which is fed through a number of conduits into different pipes which speak with a voice, and which make a harmony of song.

63. = Julii Caesaris Bulengeri (the Jesuit Jules-César Boulenger, 1558–1628). *De circo romano*, and *De theatro*. Boulenger differentiated between games explicitly according to their location and implicitly to current acceptability, but divided them between the circus or amphitheater (for sport and combats) and theaters (for dramatic performances), allocating one treatise to each.

64. = Jacques Daléchamps (Jacobus Dale Champius, 1513–1588), French writer on medicine and botany, and commentator on Pliny's *Natural History*.

65. = Claudius Salmasius (Claude de Saumaise, 1588–1653), *Claudii Salmasii Plinianæ Exercitationes*.

66. Voetius's 1663 edition corrects this to chapter 27.

1 | PROFESSORS

With respect to the predicate, since it can be asked whether the music of the organ is either necessary or useful and convenient, or at least tolerated, and whether formally its performance and function is religious worship, or at least its support. We know this beforehand, and we presuppose this; we do not explain the definition of religion, religious etc., likewise public worship or church worship, etc., [or] finally, of the worship and the church of the Old and New Testaments.

§2. We put forth now partly hypotheses and postulates, some givens[67] or data; lest while the Papists attack us, or defend their ancient and inherited customs[68] against our reformation, they occupy themselves with a mock battle against shadows. Therefore, these ideas are: I. that all divine worship, particularly that which takes place in church, or public exercises of piety, must be established from the will of God revealed in the Word; and consequently that all self-imposed religion[69] is forbidden. Concerning which see the commentators on Colossians 2, Matthew 15, and the writers of *The Common Topics*,[70] and the adversaries of the papacy, concerning traditions, concerning established worship and concerning superstition, concerning ceremonies, etc. [1663 Voetius adds: Compare the things which we are discussing above concerning liturgies and rituals, and part 3 of the selected disputations about superstition, rosaries, etc.] II. That the mode of external and ecclesiastical worship, rituals, formalities, supports, must be carried out according to the example of the apostolic church, and certainly not of any other after the times of the apostles; and that they are as much safer and more perfect, as they approach more closely to the example of that original simplicity. III. That there is not the same reasoning for private and solitary devotion and for public or church worship as regards the formalities of gestures, voice, groans, etc. and also even supports and occasions. IV. That sacred music objectively, or as far as it concerns the material, is not essentially[71] holy or religious, but becomes profane and sinful for everyone who does not follow it [sacred music] with a devout and pious spirit and conduct. V. That music, not only

---

67. διδόμενα.

68. ἤθη sua ἀρχαῖα & πατροπαράδοτα.

69. ἐθελοθρησκείαν. See Colossians 2:23.

70. = Philip Melanchthon (1497–1560), *Loci communes rerum theologicarum.* See locus 21 (*Human Ceremonies in the Church*), especially the section on *adiaphora.*

71. *formaliter.*

vocal but also instrumental, even dubious[72] music or that in which the content is not sacred, can be an occasion and motive for someone through which the mind and emotions may rise to God, by means of a certain reason in common with all other creatures and their powers and actions. Nevertheless, it should not be made part of worship on that account, or a permanent, perpetual, regular and consecrated support for worship. V. [sic. = VI] That one must not make use of all things which are permissible; even less should one apply pressure about them or introduce them anew. VI. [sic. = VII[73]] That one should abstain from every occasion, every appearance of evil, if the matter in itself and by itself is not necessary or useful. VII. [sic. = VIII] That a stumbling block should not be caused for anybody, even the least; especially in the use of something that is considered *adiaphora*. Commentaries should be consulted on 1 Corinthians 8 and 10 and on Matthew 18, and also the writers of *The Common Topics* concerning the stumbling block, and furthermore, the learned tracts by English and Scottish theologians ([Robert] Parker, Ames,[74] and other anonymous writers) speaking against certain ceremonial relics concerning the cross, genuflection, the altar, etc. VIII. [sic. = IX] That with regard to all holy and ecclesiastical exercises (namely, prayers and hymns) devotion is asked for, which is not just a potential[75] one, but actual[76] and essential;[77] not just a fleeting and spontaneous one, but stable, constant, and intentionally[78] maintained. See our *Ascetica*,[79] the discussion on *Meditation* and *Devotion*. These are indeed the hypotheses and postulates, which we put forth and establish principally from [the Lutherans,] those who have separated from the Papacy; and their teachings defend organ music in divine worship, yet are not sufficiently in agreement. We add now these very few given things,[80] which we freely concede, nor do we cause a controversy for anyone concerning these things: I. That the proper and moderate use of music for proper enjoyment is permitted. II. That [use is permitted] even

---

72. ἄδηλον.
73. From here forward the number error is corrected in the 1663 printing.
74. = William Ames (1576–1633), *Fresh Suit Against Human Ceremonies*, 430.
75. *virtualem*.
76. *actualem*.
77. *formalem*.
78. Reading *ex professo* for *ex profesto*.
79. Spiritual Exercises.
80. διδόμενα.

of music that is extremely virtuosic or ornamented, both instrumental and vocal. III. That such music even works to the glory of God; and it must be restored to this purpose, along with all of our other actions pertaining to natural or civil life. 1 Corinthians 10:31. III. [sic. = IV] That it even is, or can become, an occasion (sometimes and somewhere, whether far away or near) of lifting the mind and spirit to God. IV. [sic. = V] That properly musical short melodies, which are to be performed by voice and instrument, become fit for holy words and things. V. [sic. = VI] That such music, either purely instrumental or a combination [of voices and instruments], can be used in private by someone who has understanding, whenever he can take the time, or when he, along with David (Psalm 57:8[81]), has a ready heart, and it is for expressing or arousing spiritual feelings. VI. [sic. = VII] That it is possible that when someone hears a concert of brass instruments or of organs, or any instrumental melody whatever, and by the occurrence of a harmonious melody he is reminded of a psalm or hymn for which he perceives that this melody is suitable—then I say that he can use it on this occasion of recollection, for outbursts of meditations, aspirations, songs of praise, etc. as he freely pours them forth. Nevertheless, let him not bind his conscience in such a way by these observances, or fabricate something sacramental from it, or a mystic ritual, or anything similar. VII. [sic. = VIII] That a concert of organs, horns, clarions,[82] pipes, brass, and any other instruments whatever, can be set up and exhibited in public places, by the generosity either of the magistrates or of private men whose interests bring it about, for the honest and shared pleasure of both the citizens and visitors, which is its general, proper, and primary goal. Also [this can be done] for sacred and religious pleasures and occasions, which is a particular and secondary use, with respect to some people and some music—certainly, when the sound of the melody of a psalm or some other sacred song is seen to be set to music, and that setting of both the melody and the words has fallen to a equally knowledgeable person, and furthermore it now takes hold of a heart which has been separated for a little while from other ordinary and proper cares, and which at that time has been aroused continually, or at least at intervals, by some spiritual touch and inspiration. VIII [sic. = IX] That it is allowable in any places whatever, both at ordinary and extraordinary times, to present such musical settings.

---

81. *paratum cor meum* is in Psalm 56:8 in the Vulgate, but the modern Psalter has the equivalent passage in Psalm 57:7.

82. *lituorum*.

Only, let such a one control and moderate the exercise of his own freedom by the law of charity and prudence, so that people can distinguish clearly enough those musical pleasures from religious worship and church activities. But let more necessary public business, whether sacred or secular, not be hindered by these [pleasures].

§3. Now the position of the controversy must be set forth, and once that has been skillfully established, controversies can be easily defined. Therefore the question is, whether instrumental music or the sound of the organ, either separately or combined with vocal music, is either a necessary or at least a useful part of public worship in church; or whether it is either a part, or an action, of religion; or at least a condition, requirement, medium, or support of religion that would be practiced publicly or communally in the New Testament church, and therefore by divine law. And *First*, just as they consecrated comedies, their own diversions, the gentiles also consecrated to their own gods the sound of instruments, and brought them into temples and holy places. For all diversions in Greece were athletic, or musical, or theatrical. Musical diversions or contests were filled with songs to the gods, or hymns, and also laments, paeans, and dithyrambs; as it is in the writings of Plato at the end of book 3 of *On Laws*.[83] [Voetius adds: Proclus in his *Chrestomathy*[84] (which survives in Photius's *Bibliotheca*, book 239) numbers three kinds of lyric poetry, of which some concern the gods, some concern human beings, and some concern disasters which happened by chance. To the first class he assigns the hymn, prosodion,[85] paean,[86] dithyramb,[87] nome,[88] adonidia,[89] iobacchus,[90] hyporcheme.[91] Whoever has the time may look up the descriptions of those things there.] In short, all of ancient music was divine,[92] dear to the gods; and all knowledge of it was as-

---

83. That is, his dialogue Νόμοι.

84. Voetius incorrectly referred to Proclus's work as *Chrestomachy*. It is *Chrestomathy*. Proclus's third category was lyrics addressed to both gods and humans, and he mentioned a fourth division dealing with "various occasions" (προσπιπτούσας περιστάσεις).

85. προσόδιον, processional.

86. παιᾶνα, a song of triumph originally addressed to Apollo or Artemis.

87. διθύραμβον, choral song in honor of the wine god Dionysus.

88. νόμον, ancient Greek music for either solo instrumental or voice accompanied by an instrument.

89. ἀδωνίδια, Adonis-poems.

90. ἰόβακχον, Bacchus-hymn.

91. ὑπορχήματα, songs accompanied by movements.

92. Heimbergius writes *erat* ("was"), as translated here. But Voetius altered to

1 | PROFESSORS

signed either to the honor of the gods or to the education of the young, with Plutarch as witness in his *Concerning Music* in which a complaint is made that this effeminate and theatrical [music] is all too far removed from music which is obviously religious. [Voetius adds: However, all of the dramatic theater, along with all other diversions and spectacles, had been dedicated[93] to the honor and worship of the gods, and it took a part in that; therefore theatrical music did so too. See also Exodus 32, with 1 Corinthians 14:7–8, and Tertullian, *On Games*, chapter 10: "Indeed, by what vocal sound, and modes, and organs, and lyres, they are transfixed," etc. In Daniel 3:5, the custom of idolaters is plainly shown, where all are commanded to celebrate the dedication and worship of the image, and when the sound of horns, the flute, cithara, etc. was heard.] Further, concerning the theatrical [music], and so also the entire music of the ancients, and the musical instruments, one can see those things which Jules-César Boulenger studiously collected in his second book *Concerning Theater*. *Second*, just like the Jews of today, they judge that the entire Old Testament external mode of divine worship must be retained as sometimes figurative, sometimes changeable; so also the sacred music which is described in 1 Chronicles 25. Let me not say anything about the gentile affections[94] of the ancients Jews before Christ, an example of which they were providing in the funeral rites in Matthew 9:23. [Voetius adds: where the flute-players[95] are remembered. On gentile funeral music, see Gutherius, book 1, chapter 23 of *De Jure Manium*,[96] the commentators on Persius's *Satire* 3, and the notes on Matthew 9:29 of Pricaeus.[97] The Jews not only imitated this custom of the gentiles, but also later retained the practice as if it were a law; if indeed this can be believed of the Talmudic Mishnah in the tractate *Ketubot*, chapter 4 section 4:[98] Rabbi Yehuda said that "*even a poor man among the Israelites shall not provide*" [Voetius adds: "*evidence for his wife who has died in captivity*[99] *fewer than* שני חלילים ומקיגגת, [that is,] *two flutes and a female mourner.*"

---

dicebatur ("was called").

93. Reading *dedicatum* for *dedicatus*.
94. κακοζηλία.
95. αὐληταί.
96. = Jacobus Gutherius (Jacques Goutière or Gouthier, 1568–1638), *De jure manium*.
97. = John Price (1600?–1676), *Critici Sacri*.
98. Actually, chapter 4, section 46b:3.
99. Voetius's parenthetical insert ("evidence for his wife who has died in captivity") is misleading. Voetius has confused Rabbi Yehuda's saying with the Talmud's discussion,

Maimonides repeats the same thing in the same words in חושיא[100] chapter 14, where he adds: "If he is rich, let everything be done in proportion to his worth." Nebrissensis in his *Quinquagena*,[101] chapter 46 on the cited passage in Matthew, observes that flutes were commonly brought in for the funerals of boys and girls, according to that saying of Statius in the *Thebaid*, book 6: "*the flute, with which it is the custom to lead forth the young shades*"; and for grown men, trumpets, according to that passage in Persius *Satire* 3:[102] "*Hence the trumpet, torches*," etc.; and the comment of Lactantius, which he cites in the same place; and from him, Johannes Drusius[103] [cites it] in the *Praeterita*. Tertullian in *De Spectaculis*,[104] chapter 10, calls the flutes and trumpets two of the most impure influencers of funerals and holy rites. In his *Notes* on Matthew chapter 9:23, Grotius[105] seems to want to excuse this meaningless funeral

in a previous sentence, of the duty of ransoming one's wife from captivity. The context shows that the provision of the flutes and female mourner was considered the minimal required duty for any wife's burial. The Talmud in context actually mentions the duty of ransoming one's wife from captivity, and that the provision of flutes and female mourners was the minimal required duty for any wife's burial.

100. *Mishneh Torah*, the Hebrew letters probably indicate the heading title. However, although laws about mourning are discussed there, and mourning and walking before the bier are mentioned, Voetius' citations do not appear. Perhaps this is because the Latin "M." is an indication that the edition was in progress at that time.

101. = Antonius Nebrissensis, (Antonio de Nebrija, 1444?–1522), *In Quinquaginta Sacrae Scripturae*.

102. *Satire* 3, I.103.

103. = Johannes van den Driesche (1550–1616), *Annotationum*.

104. *On the Games*.

105. = Hugo Grotius (Huigh de Groot, 1583–1645). *Annotations in Novum Testamentum*, 104: *Tibias in luctu usitatas apud Iudaeos etiam Iosephus Belli Iudaici lib. III nos docet. Puto etiam falli eos qui à profanis gentibus morem hunc ad Hebraeos putant deductum. Recte enim ab aliis demonstratum est, exstare in antiquissimis Hebraeorum scriptis ejus moris vestigia; sicut & praeficarum mentio est apud Ieremiam ix, 17. ñeque vero in Lege ulla ejus rei interdictio invenitur. Denique tota pompa funeralis non novitium erat inventum, sed Abrahami, Isaaci, Iacobi, Iofephi exemplo nitebatur. Quo convicitur Taciti error putantis curam corporis, moremque condendi magis quàm cremandi, ab Ægyptiis ad Iudaeos pervenisse. Apparet enim ex Sacra historia multó ante quàm Hebraei in Ægyptum immigrassent eundem morem ab ipsorum majoribus usurpatum. Vero autem simile est ritus funerales, praesertim vero humandorum corporum morem (qui apud omnes gentes crematione est antiquior) originem habere a primis post Diluvium temporibus, ad detestationem* ἀνθρωποφαγίας *[morís edendi humanas carnes], quae inter caetera extremae feritatis scelera pristinum orbem invaserat*. Josephus indeed teaches us (*Bell. Iud.* book III) that among the Jews, pipes were used to express grief. Indeed, I believe that they err who believe that this custom was taken from the profane races to the Hebrews. For rightly it was demonstrated by others that the traces of this custom exist in the most ancient writings

1 | PROFESSORS

procession, when he says that it had not been forbidden in the law of God. To this end, he decides that this custom was not brought over from the gentiles to the Jews, but was very ancient among them. However, this is not at all proven about flutes or other instrumental music. That passage of Jeremiah 9:17, selected by him, indicates some antiquity (some centuries before Christ) for hired women mourners, not for flutes; but it does not really indicate the most ancient kind, as in the families of the patriarchs or before the Israelites went to Egypt. And Scripture is a frequent witness that certainly, in the time of Jeremiah and the entire time of the kings, and even that of the judges, due to some sort of bad imitation,[106] empty observances and superstitions, nay, even the grossest idolatry,[107] had been transferred from the gentiles to the Israelites. Nor can anyone ignore this who has looked even slightly at the ancient records of that nation. As for what he says about a funeral procession, that it is not an invented novelty but supported[108] by the example of Abraham, Isaac, Jacob, and Joseph, this cannot apply to flutes and hired women mourners more than to the gashing of the flesh, which in Leviticus 19[109] is forbidden.] Third, because in the inferior and very corrupt ages this almost theatrical music had gradually and imperceptibly[110] crept into their churches and sacred rites, the Papists[111] are compelled now to defend it, or at least to excuse it, lest their church should seem to have been in want of some reformation. Its use, however is 1. In canonical hours, or the divine office, which is publicly completed in churches; namely, in solemn vespers. 2. In celebration of feasts, whether those have been established and ordinary, or are

---

of the Hebrews; just as there is also mention of hired female mourners in Jeremiah 9:17, nor is there found any prohibition of this thing in the Law. Finally, the notion of a funeral procession had been founded not for the sake of newness, but it depended upon the examples of Abraham, Isaac, Jacob, and Joseph. Thus the error of Tacitus is refuted, who thought that care for a corpse and the custom of burial rather than cremation came to the Jews from the Egyptians. For it appears from the Sacred History that this custom was adopted from their ancestors long before the Hebrews had immigrated into Egypt. But it is also likely that funeral rites, and especially the custom of burying human remains (which among all peoples is more ancient than cremation) has its origin in the first ages after the flood, in revulsion against cannibalism (the custom of eating human flesh), which had invaded the ancient world among the other crimes of extreme ferocity.

106. κακοζηλία.
107. Voetius has *idolkakzerolatriam*, but it should be spelled *idolkakozelatriam*.
108. Reading *subnixam* for *subnizem*.
109. Leviticus 19:28.
110. *sensim sine sensu* is a quotation from the end of Cicero's *De Senectute*, section 38.
111. *pontificii*, same word as for pagan priests.

extraordinary eucharistic days, when they resound, in the customary way, with the *Te Deum Laudamus*.[112] 3. In the celebration of solemn Mass, which therefore because of its vocal and instrumental music is both commonly and distinctly called *een singende Misse*, that is, a *sung Mass*.[113] How much secularity, however, has grown together with those organs (just as a special divine malediction usually accompanies all human self-willed religion,[114] we ourselves shall not say; but we send the reader to the Papists themselves: Cajetan in his *Summula* on the word *Organon*, p. 519, and in 22. question 91, article 1; and in the same place George of Venice[115] disputation 6, question 9; Bartholomew Fumus[116] in *Armilla*, "organ"; Viguerus *Institutes*, page 62;[117]

112. *We Praise You, O God.*
113. Literally, a *singing Mass*.
114. εθελοθρησκείαν. See Colossians 2:23.
115. = Gregorio de Valencia (1549?–1603), *Gregorii de Valentia Metimnensis . . . Commentariorum theologicorum tomi 4. In quibus omnes quaestiones, quae continentur in Summa theologica D. Thomae Aquinatis, ordine explicantur ac suis etiam in locis controuersiae omnes fidei elucidantur Tomus primus quartus . . . Cum variis indicibus* (Lugduni: Horatij Cardon, 1619) 1416: *Ad excitandum*, inquit, *interiorem affectum tum proprium tum etiam aliorum, praesertim vulgarium, qui interdum adeo infirmi sunt, ut non modo vocum cantu, sed etiam organis et musicis instrumentis ad sensum rerum spiritualium concitandi sint.*

116. = Bartholomaeus Fumus (Fumum, or Fumo, ?–1545), *Summa aurea armilla*, 671: ORGANUM
Organorum usus in ecclesia est licitus, licet Romana ecclesia coram pontifice eis non utatur, non tamen licet inter divina, in eis canere vel pulsare seculares cantus, vel plausus, aut turpes, & amatoria[s] cantilenas, & est mortale, sec[undum] Caie[tanum] ibi, in Summa. Est enim contrarium divino officio, cuius est excitare devotionem, & tales conatus excitant ad turpia, vel vana. Similiter qui tales conducunt sonatores, & consentiunt eis in hoc, possent hi aliquo modo excusari, quando crederent non esse prohibitum, cum in aliis ecclesiis sic fieret. Sed a sono turpium nulla ignorantia excusat, quia statim continent contrarietatem ad solennitatem Christi, secundum Caieta[num].ibi, in summa, supra, Cantus.§.4.
The use of organs in church has been permitted, although the Roman church does not use them in the presence of the pontiff. However, it is not permitted, in the midst of religious activities, to sing or play on them secular songs or noisy pieces, or shameful and amorous popular songs; and that is mortal sin, according to Cajetan in the *Summa*, in the place above ["Cantus," section 4]. For it is contrary to the divine office, the task of which is to arouse devotion; but such efforts as those arouse shameful or vain things. Similarly, those who employ such musicians and consent to their doing this, can in some way be excused when they believed that this was not prohibited, since it was done that way in other churches. But no ignorance is an excuse for the sound of shameful things, because they instantly involve an opposition to the solemn celebration of Christ, according to Cajetan in the *Summa*, in the place above, "Cantus" section 4.

117. = Jean Viguier (1527–1550), *Instituiones ad Christianam Theologiam*, 197: *Quia secundum diversas melodias sonorum animi hominum diversimodè disponuntur. Ubi verò*

1 | PROFESSORS

Erasmus,[118] in notes on 1 Corinthians 14 and in the *Apologia* for them against Alberto Pio[119] titled *Concerning Song* page 127, where he [Erasmus] says, *in the chapel of the Pope such vocal chattering* (so he calls polyphonic[120] music) *is heard, yet almost never a sermon. Such chattering also heard as well at the court of the Emperor and of other kings.* Add Navarrus in *Manual* chapter 12, section 87, and the *Treatise concerning Prayers and the Hours*, chapter 17; the same Council of Trent session 22 where [there is discussion] concerning things to be avoided in the celebration of Mass; Thomas Sanchez in his *Praecepta Decalogi*,[121] book 2, chapter 37; and especially Lindanus in his *Panoply*, book 4 chapter 78.[122] We are not going to set down here his words and those of the rest of them, leaving the investigation of the authors, whom I selected in good faith, to the industry of any reader. Further the Jesuit Bayllius defends this use of organs in his catechism, part 2 question 36;[123] and Cajetan in

---

ex voce, cantu, vel organis, non excitatur devotio, sed tædium crescit ex labore, vel ignorātia, cantus, vel nimia melodia animus ad voluptates carnales trahitur: omnia hmōi exteriora signa omittĕda sunt.

118. = Desideradus Erasmus (1466–1536). His commentary on 1 Corinthians 14 is found in *Desiderrii Erasmi Opera Omnia*, VI:731C–32C.

119. = Alberto Pio (Pium, or Pii, "the pious," Prince of Carpi, 1475–1531) who challenged Erasmus on church music. *Ad Erasmi Roterodami expostulationem*, 259: *Nihil scurrilitatis, nihil ludicri, nihil indecorum caerimoniis sacris misceatur, sed omnia sint gravia, verenda et rationi consentanea ac divinae maiestati convenientia, quae aedificant, non destruant, mentem ad divina convertant, non distrahant, inflammant, non infrigident* [refrigident], *breviter in id accommodentur ad quod fuerunt instituta, nihil secus, nihil perperam fiat. Nam licent* [etsi] *cunctis fere in rebus quaedam minus recte minusque decenter fieri contingat, in sacris tamen omnia decentissime et reverentissime praestare, quantum* [quam] *maxime fieri possit, est enitendum utque nulli aut minimi permittantur abusus et sicubi prava consuetudo inducta fuerit aboleatur. Quae cura et solicitudo ad eos in primis pertinent qui sacris praesunt. Quamobrem, ut dicam quod sentio, non valde probandus mihi esse videtur usus tam frequens perfracti cantus, quo variae voces exaudiuntur, verba percipi non possunt, nec tantus strepitus organorum.*

120. πολύφωνον.

121. = Tomás Sánchez (1550–1610), *Opus morale in praecepta Decalogi.*

122. = Guilelmus Damasus Lindanus (Van der Lindt, 1525–1588), *Panoplia evangelica*, 572: *Quamquam non me fugiat, quibusdam musicam cum organis & musicis rectius videri retinendam, quibus equidem perlibenter assentiar, si una pro isto musices genere, quod nunc passim Ecclesias occupat, aliud introducatur, et gravius, et rebus ipsis convenientius, et si non, ut oportet, pronuntiationi, quam cantui vicinius, saltem rebus, quae canuntur, aptius atque accommodatius.*

123. = Guillaume Baile, (1557–1620), *Controversiarum Catechismus*, 165: *Propheta Regius non semper ore, Dei laudes depromebat, sed subindex etiam in Cithara, sicuti suorum psalmorum ultimo nos exhortatur, ut in sono tubae; in psalterio & cithara; in tympano & choro; in chordis & organo; in Cymbalis jubilationis, & his similibus musicorum*

his *Summula* weakly excuses the same, rather than defending it; and after him, Fumus in the places cited, [defends] what naturally may be allowed; and Suarez[124] in volume 2 *Concerning Religion*, treatise 4, book 4, chapter 8, defends it more timidly yet: *That music is neither wicked in itself nor simply prohibited by ecclesiastical law*. More audaciously, the *Episcopale* or *Ceremoniale Episcoporum*[125] book I, chapter 28, says: *It is proper for the music of the organ and musicians to be used in church, on all Sundays of course, and on feast days* (with some exceptions) *etc., and whenever the bishop, about to celebrate a solemn Mass, enters the church, or when he departs, having completed the divine service, etc. Likewise at the entrance of an apostolic representative, cardinal, archbishop, or other bishop, etc. until the aforesaid have prayed, and divine service has begun. At Matins which are solemnly celebrated on greater feast days, etc.* In the same place he adds how often and when the organ should be played either for accompaniments[126] or alternately, etc. Look there [i.e. in the *Ceremoniale*] for such pieces of nonsense. Cornelius á Lapide,[127] in a marginal note on 1 Corinthians 14, says that music is recommended for three reasons;[128] but in the context itself[129] he makes no other argument against the opinion of Cajetan than: *But now the practice of Christians holds the contrary:*

---

instrumentis mirablia Dei resonare faciamus. Unde nostros Reformatos mirror tam parum divinis paginis conformiter egisse, tam parum antiquissimae consuetudini; imo & fuorum in Anglia Conreformatorum praxi, organa & regalia destruendo, tribuisse. Quod obijciunt ex I. Corinth. c. 14. v. 16. Idiotam non posse respondere Amen, *quia licet verborum sonum audiat, sensum tamen eorundem non penetrat: respondemus sanctum Paulum illo capita fere loqui de exhortationibus, de collationibus spiritualibus, nec non de antiquis Sancis, quorum commemoratione, in omni se Christiani conservabant pietate.*

124. = Francisco Suarez (1548–1617), *Operis de Religione*, 194.

125. The *Caeremoniale episcoporum* demands that where instruments other than the organ are to be used, permission must be sought from the bishop. This liturgical book was first published as binding for the Universal Church by Pope Clement VIII, in 1600, and has passed through many editions to the present day. Heimenbergius's reference (*Organs are used in the church every Sunday and annual festival*) omitted this sentence that followed: *They must not be played during Advent nor during Lent until Easter except for the third Sunday of Advent, the fourth Sunday of Lent, and the festivals which occur during these times.*

126. *consequentibus*

127. = Cornelis Cornelissen van den Steen (1567–1637), *Commentaria in sacram Scripturam*, 264. Lapide wrote a commentary on all books of the Catholic canon of scripture, including the deuterocanonical ones, except for Job and Psalms.

128. Note that Heimenbergius doesn't list these three reasons!

129. That is, in the text itself as opposed to a marginal note.

so that, with David, they constantly make use of organs and music in worship;[130] and page 110.5: *In short, this is approved by the Church's practice: for in nearly all the Christian world this tradition either is approved, or tolerated, etc.* With this statement he clearly implies that in his inner conscience he is not able to contradict Cajetan. [Voetius adds: In the commentary on Sirach 32, and on Exodus 15, he[131] seems to speak more openly.] Lorinus's[132] *Commentary on Wisdom*, chapter 19, and before him Johann Stephan Durant, book I *On the Rites of the Church*, book 1, chapter 13,[133] [and] Demochares *Concerning celebration of the Mass*, chapter 3,[134] seem to wish to defend the view a little more confidently. [Voetius adds: Along with these people, Schulting asserts it in part 1 of *Hierarchica Anacrisis*, book II, page 148,[135] and book I, page 51;[136] in the same place he says that he has *defended organs against the Calvinists,*

---

130. *Commentarii in Scripturam Sacram* (Lugduni: Pelaguad, 1854), "Commentaria in 1. Epist. Ad Corinthios, Cap. XIV." Vol IX, 329: *Sed usus jam Christianorum habet contrarium, ut cum Davide ad excitandam devotionem populi, qui æque vocem Latinam non intelligeret, organis subinde et musica in sacris utantur, idque.*

131. That is, Cornelius á Lapide.

132. = Johannes Lorinus (Jean de Lorini, 1559–1634), *Commentarius in Sapientiam*, 683ff.

133. = Ioannes Stephanus Duranti (Jean-Etienne Durand, 1534–1589), *De ritibus ecclesiae catholicae*, I:13:34: *Plenè Democares de observanda Missarum Celebrat. cap. 14. Organorum usum Ecclesia, ait, Synodus Senonens. cap. 17. ad cultum, & servitium Divinum recepit: modo nihil praeter hymnos divinos, & cantica spiritualia organa repraesentent.*

134. = Antonio Monchiaceno Demochare Ressonaeo (Antoine de Mouchy, 1494–1574), *Missarum Celebratione*, 41ff.

135. = Cornelius Schulting (1540–1604), *Hierarchica Anacrisis*, II:148: *De Interrogatione 34. Eadem vide in Dordoracena Articulo 50, ratio huius canonis illis esse videtur, quod Paulus (I. Corinth. 14) docere videatur organa esse tollenda. Respondemus cum Reuerendissimo Lindano in Admonitione de Idolis fugiendis, folio 22, "non est creadendum Paulum Davidi aut Helisaeo refragari, cum tali cultu spiritum ad coelestia erigat & animos excitet ac promoveat." De Organis lege Speculum Langhecrucii de canonicis & divinis officiis, & Joannem Stephanum Durantem libro 1 de Ritibus Catholicae ecclesiae cap. 13. de Organis Prolixè in meo Prochiro MS. De divinis officiis de Organis. Politia ecclesiastica Herbornensis libro 1. capite 13 de divnis officiis de Organis.*

136. *De organis retinendis contra Calvinistas dixi Tomo 4. Bibliothecae Sanctae, Parte 2 in confutationem Synodorum Belgicarum contra can[onem] 50 Consilii Dordaraceni. De antiquitate Organorum lege etiam Joannem Durantem de Ritibus Catholicae ecclesiae, l. 1 c. 13., vide pulcherrima apud Langherucium in Speculo Canonicor[um] c. 32., Concilium Tridentinum sessione 22. de observandis in celebratione Missae, eas musicas arcet ab ecclesia, quae sive organo, sive cantu lascivum quid aut impurum admiscent, proinde aliam musicam instrumentalem honestam et pudicam as castam admittere et approbare judicatur censeturque. Schulting, Hierarchica, I:51.*

especially against Zepper[137] *and the synods of Dordrecht and Middelburg, in volume 4 of the* Bibliotheca [Ecclesiastica],[138] *part*[139] *2, on the confutation of the Dutch*[140] *synods, and in his* Handbook,[141] part 2. Likewise in book II, page 148, he commends Langhecrucius in the *Mirror concerning Canonical and*

137. = Wilhelm Zepper (1550–1607).

138. Schulting, *Bibliotheca Ecclesiastica catholica*, IV:2:113: *Canone 50 Organorum usum ex templis eliminandum decernunt. Idem statuunt cap. 35 Synhodi Nationalis, usus organorum, aiunt, praesertim ante concionem non probandus. Ideoque paulatim et successive abolendus. Idem Canone 54 Synhodi Middleburgensis repetunt. Canoni 50 Dordoracenae causam Organorum tollendorum addunt, quod Paulus 1 Corinth.14 ita doceat. Sed D. [divus] Paulus Davidi aut Elizaeo non est putandus refragari, qui ex Dei Spiritu istum etiam divinae religionis cultum non parum animos ad coelestia erigentem & excitantem promoveat. Verum graviorem sibi causam adferre videntur, cur haec sint prorsus abolenda, quod hoc decretum, inquiunt isti, utile fuerit, ut in oblivionem veniant, quae antea populus audivit. Hoc est, ut omnis Dei ac rerum divinarum memoria quae in organis ac canticis Deo canuntur, semel de mentibus hominum aboleatur, atque obliti Dei patrum suorum novum Calvini aut alterius haeresiarchae idolum suscipiant, venerentur, colant.* In Canon 50 they decree that the use of organs be eliminated from churches. They establish the same thing in chapter 35 of the National Synod; the use of organs (they say) must not be approved, particularly before assembling together. And therefore, gradually and successively, it must be abolished. They repeat the same thing in canon 54 of the Synod of Middelburg. To Dordt's Canon 50 they add a reason for taking away organs away: because Paul teaches in this way in 1 Corinthians 14. But holy Paul, who must not be thought of as contradicting David or Elisha [2 Kings 3:15], would also, by the Spirit of God, promote this worship, which belongs to God's religion, and which greatly elevates and arouses souls to heavenly things [this argument comes from Lindanus, according to the *Hierarchica* passage *De interrogatione 34*, above]. In truth, they seem to impart to themselves a more serious reason why these things should be abolished: because this decree (they say) would be useful for bringing to oblivion those things which the people have formerly listened to—that is, so that every remembrance of God and of divine things, for which music is made to God by instruments and by singing, may be blotted out once for all for the minds of humanity, and that, having forgotten the God of their ancestors, they might receive, venerate and worship a new idol, one of Calvin's or of some other heresiarch. [Schulting then discusses the use of bells and, interestingly, ends: *De origine organorum musicorum in templis, fortasse, si vitam superstitem Deus largietur, ex professo aliquando istos libros confutandos mihi sumam. Hoc duntaxat jam affirmo, quicunque adjumenta & instrumenta promovendi cultus divini abolent, eos Sathanae & Antichristo viam sternere.* Concerning the origin of musical instruments in churches: perhaps, if God grants me to survive, I will take it upon myself someday to confute those books. At any rate, I am affirming this now: whoever abolishes these aids and means for advancing the worship of God is preparing the way for Satan and the Antichrist.]

139. Reading *secundo* for *sancto*.

140. *Beligicaru*.

141. *Prochiro MS* (= draft manuscript or handbook in manuscript). Perhaps referring to Schulting's *Opus variarum lectionum et animadversionum adversus lib. I. Instit. Jo. Calvini* (n.p., n.d.), a manuscript that has not survived.

1 | PROFESSORS

Divine Offices.[142]] Bellarmine mutters very anxiously on behalf of the organ music now habitually used in the papacy in *Concerning Good Works in Particular*, book I, chapter 16 and 17. In discussing the status of the controversy he does not dare mention organs even once, but by trickery and cunning he argues against us, and approves many things about sacred music in general: only in the course of the disputation, in passing[143] and on a given occasion, does he even remember organs, as things *which may be naturally brought to the worship of God*: however, his conscience was stinging him so that he ends with this feeble conclusion on page 2686 (of the octavo edition): *On account of those in church who are weak it should be retained.* [Voetius adds: Learn from his own words how inconsistent Raphael la Torre[144] is in question 22, article 91, disputation 1, as follows: *I say in the first place: In the Church of Christ, that is, in the divine offices, there was no frequent use of actual musical instruments, as of the lyre, the harp and of other similar means for singing divine praises,* etc., where it cites, in the same place, Augustine on Psalm 32, and Justin Martyr on question 107, etc. A second reason is taken from Master Thomas [Aquinas], *from the Philosopher* [Aristotle] *in the Politics, viii,*[145] which is to be set forth in this fashion: "*Musical instruments of this sort move the mind toward pleasure, rather than forming some good state of mind, drawn*

---

142. = Jan van Langekruys (Langecruys, ?–1569): *De malorum horum*. Schulting's commendation: *Eadem vide in Dordoracena Articulo 50, ratio huius canonis illis esse videtur, quod Paulus (1 Corinth. 14) docere videatur organa esse tollenda. Respondemus cum Reverendissimo Lindano in* Admonitione de Idolis fugiendis, *folio 22, "non est credendum Paulum Davidi aut Heliaeo refragari, cum talis cultus spiritum ad coelestia erigat & animos excitat ac promoveat."* (Heirarcha 2:148). See the same things in Dordrecht's Article 50; the reason for this canon appears to be that Paul seems to teach that instruments should be taken away. We answer, together with the most reverend Lindanus in the *Admonition on Fleeing Idols*, folio 22: "it is not to be believed that Paul contradicts David or Elisha, since such a worship lifts up souls toward heavenly things, and both arouses and enlarges them."

143. ἐν παρόδῳ, see 1 Corinthians 16:7.

144. = Francisco de Turrianus (Raphael de la Torre[s],1509–1584), *De partibus potentialibus*.

145. This quotation is not from Aristotle's Politica viii:6, but from Aquinas's commentary on Aristotle's Politics viii:6. The Latin quoted here is an expansion of the text in *Summa Theologiae* 2a.2ae.91 [the Second Part of the Second Part, Question 91, Article 2, Reply to Objection 4]: *For such like musical instruments move the soul to pleasure rather than create a good disposition within it*. But what Aristotle is writing about is the education of the young, which is a different context. Aristotle wrote: *Flutes must not be introduced into education, nor any other professional instrument, such as the harp or any other of that sort, but such instruments as will make them good listeners either at their musical training or in their other lessons.*

toward devotion and for the formation of good character," etc. I say in the second place, and indirectly, the previously mentioned musical instruments can excite us to pious emotions by leading us to devotion and settled character. For this reason, their use has not been completely banished from the Church, but it should be sparingly accepted, and not increased: for these instruments, which in themselves are useless for any purpose, and useful only by chance, must be used rarely and sparingly. Thus flutes (Spanish ministrils[146]) should be used with moderation in the great celebrations. It must be said otherwise concerning the use of organs: on account of the gravity and dignity of the instrument, and on account of the advantages which the churches' singers receive when they are played, their use has been accepted by the Church at this time and applied only to sacred things, although, as Cajetan reports, this instrument never is played before the Pope. Concerning which Cajetan notes two things. First, that at the time of Master Thomas [Aquinas] there was no use of organs. Second, that one must beware lest abuses creep in during this playing, abuses which we said can be found in song, and so on. However, the first [comment of Cajetan] is not expressly contained in Blessed Thomas: perhaps in his time the use of these instruments was rare, which for this reason is said to be "no use," or because the use was recognized by only a few. Nonetheless, Julian (who is much older than Master Gregory on chapter 32 of Job) proves that the use of organs is not recent; and many others whom Durand cites in On the Rites of the Church, *book I chapter 13. Therefore, the answer to the argument that Peter Martyr disapproves of the use of organs and church music is that Christians are not bound to reject all the rituals of the Jews. For they retain the tithe, the offering of first fruits, and many other traditions: but they are bound to reject only those which were figures of some mystery of Christ who was yet to come, such as the eating of the paschal lamb, circumcision, new moons, and sabbaths. But the uses of song and of musical instruments were not of this type but were certain means for exciting the devotion of the people. Now if some things were not indeed figurative of Christ yet to come nor of anything pertaining to that, and Christians make use of them, they should not necessarily be said to be Judaizing because of*

---

146. Castilian Spanish "ministril" (note spelling) properly means a player of flutes and other instruments, as the English word *minstrel*. De la Torre uses it to mean the instruments themselves. There probably was some confusion of meanings.

1 | PROFESSORS

that.[147]] *Fourth*,[148] among contemporary Lutherans Eckhard undertakes to defend openly, with his arguments in the *Little Collection of Controversies* chapter 21, the Latin songs, harmonious choirs, and organ music in churches.[149] [Voetius adds: Before him there were people who tried the same thing:

147. *Dico primo: In Ecclesiâ Christi non fuit frequens usus musicorum instrumentorum corporalium, ut lyrae, cytharae, & similium divinis laudibus decantandis. Ita D. Augustin. super Psalm 32 in principio, dicens cytharam ab Ecclesiae modulation esse proscriptam. Et Justinum Martyr quaestione 107. . . . Secunda ratio desumitur à D. Thom. ex philosopho 8. Polyticortum, formāda in hunc modū. Huiusmodi musica instrumenta magis animum movent ad delectatione, quam per ea formetur interiusV bonus aliquis affectus conducens ad devotionem, vel bonos formandos mores. . . . Secundo dico. Per accidens, & indirectè praefata instrumenta musica possunt excitare ad pios affectus conducentes ad devotionem & mores componendos. . . . ex quo fit ut usus eorum non sit om ninò ab Ecclesiâ relegatus, sed parcè acceptandus, nec extendendus: quia his, quæ per se inutilia sunt ad aliquem finem, & per accidens utilia, utendum est rarò, & parcè. Unde cum moderatione in magnis celebritatibus usus est tibiarum, Hispanè, Ministriles. . . . Secus dicendum est de organorum usu, qui propter gravitatem, & modestiam instrumenti, & propter commoditates, quas in eorum pulsatione cantores Ecclesiarū percipiūt iam ab Ecclesiâ acceptatus est, & solis sacris applicitus, quamuis ut refert Caieta. hic coram Summo Pontifice quam pulsentur. Circa quae Caieta. notat duo. Primū tempore D. Thom. non fuisse organorum usum. Secundum, cauendum esse, ne in his pulsandis subrepant abusus, quos in cantu diximus reperiri posse. . . . Primum autem non expresse habetur in D. Thoma: fortasse suo tempore erat rarus eorū usus, qui ob id nullus dicitur esse, aut quia à paucis agnitus: nihilominus organorū usum nō esse recentem probat Iulianus multo antiquior quàm D. Gregorius super cap. 32. Iob, & plures alii, quos citat Durantus de Ritibus Ecclesia lib. 1. c. 13. Igitur ad argumentum, quod est Petri Martyris Hæretici improbātis organorū, & cantus Ecclesiastici usum respondetur, Christianos non teneri ajbicere omnes cæremonias Iudaeorum: Nam decimationem, primitarum largitionem, & alias multas retinent, sed eas dumtaxat tenentur explodere, quæ figuræ erāt alicuius mysterii erga Christum venturum, ut esum agni Paschalis, circumcisionem, neomenias, & sabbatha; usus autem cantus, & musicorum instrumentorum non errant hujusmodi, sed media quædam ad excitandam devotionem plebis. Quod si aliqua figuralia erant non quidem Christi venturi, vel alicujus ad is pertinentis; unde non continuo, atque Christiani his utuntur, iudaïzare dicendi sunt.* De Torre, *De partibus potentialibus*, 889–90.

148. A *Fourth* heading is printed here, but there is no third. Likely the Martyr material was meant to be Voetius's third point.

149. = Henricus Eckhardus (Eckhard, 1580–1624), *Fasciculus Controversiarum*, 636–639: *Beza in Colloq. Mompelg. Parte 2. Pag. 26. Si Apostolus meritò Peregrinarum linguarum usum in coetu ecclesiaco prohibuit, Multò minùs sonos illos musicos, quibus aures solae, iis quae cantantur, nullo modo asset . Et quid amplius, annon expressis verbis, etc.*
I. Argum.
Illud, quo Deus laudatur, non est ex Ecclesia proscribendum. Cantionibus Latinis & Musicâ, tum vocali tum Organicâ Deus laudatur. Ergo.
II. Argument.
Quod Spiritus Sanctus praecipit, ejus pius & licitus est usus. Spiritus Sanctus praecipit Deum laudare Musicâ & instrumentis Musicis. Ergo. Assumpt. Psalm. 149. Laudate Deum

Jacob Andreae[150] at the Colloquy at Montbéliard, part 2; Brenz[151] in the *Homilies on Penitence*, homily 14, where in the title and the homily itself he creates a state of controversy, "about church singing, and the organ":[152] however, his reasons include nothing except church singing.] *Fifth*, there are some who defend or excuse organ music also in the Chapel Royal and the cathedral churches, just as they do for the remnants of religious rites in England. Among these is Whitgift[153] in his *Response to Admonition*, p. 206.

in chordis & Organo, laudate eum in cymbalis benè sonantibus.

III. Argum.

Quod factitatum est à piis Regibus in VT Deque approbatum, nec abrogatum, illius imitatio hodiè quoque licita est in NT Deoque approbata. At Musica & Chori Musici Harmonia à laudatißimis Regibus, Davide, Salomone, Ezechia, Iosaphato, Iosia, etc. in Templum Domini publicè introducta, Deo probabatur, 3. Reg. 10. 2. Paral. 20. Ergò ejus imitatio hodie quoque licita eset, & Deo approbata.

IV. Argument.

Quo animus hominis excitatur ad devotionem & alacritatem Spiritus, ejus in Templo non inutilis est usus. Musicâ, organis & concentibus Musuicis animus hominis excitatur ad devotionem & alacritatem Spiritus. Ergo. Assumpt. Exemplo nobis sunt Elisaeus, 2nd Reg. 3. Saul, 1st Sam. 16. Augustine qui in l. Conf. write se Musicâ Harmonia saepè adeò commotum, ut ex devotione inter canendum lachrymas profuderit, & Ambrosius, qui testatur se Musicâ sub Arianorum persecutione animum suum erexisse & non parùm confirmasse.

V. Argum.

Concentus & Harmonia Musica admonet de fraterna animorum concordia & Confessionis harmonia. Ergò Musicae Harmoniae pius est usus.

Obj. I. Beza in Actis pag 26.

Paul, 1 Cor. 14. improbat peregrinarum linguarum usum in Ecclesia. Ergò multò minùs probat sonos Harmonicos, qui non intelliguntur.

R. Paulus sermonis peregrini usum in Ecclesia non omninò rejicit, sed eos reprehendit, qui hoc dono in publicis coetibus se ostentabant & efferebant, docens, I. donum Prophetiae esse praeferendum dono linguarum, II. dono Prophetiae aedificari omnes, dono linguarum tantùm intelligents. Cantionum ergò Latinarum usus in Ecclesiis nostris damnari haud debet quia I. per illas aedificantur intelligents. II. Semper illis adjunguntur cantiones etiam germanicae, & III. usus cantionum praecipuus est, glorificatio Dei, Eph. 5th B.C. 19. cui non minùs inserviunt Latinae, quàm Germanicae cantiones.

Obj. II. Anhaldini p. 74.

Lutherus organa Musica inter Baalis insignia refert.

R. Accenset ibidem etiam templa altaria, candelas, imagines, Baptisteria, thuribula, calices, &c. non autem simpliciter, sed si singularis aliquis cultus illis affingatur.

150. = D. Jacob Andreæ (1528–1590). See Marie-Alexis Colin (ed.), *French Renaissance Music*, 455–79.

151. = Johannes Brenz (1499–1570), *De Poenitentia*, 141–53.

152. *De Cantu Ecclesiastico & Organo* is actually homily 13 (Brenz, *De Poenitentia*, 134–41).

153. = Johann Whitgistus (John Whitgift, 1530–1604), *An answer to a certen Libel*, 205–6: *Standing or sitting at this time or that time is indifferent, and therfore may both*

However, nothing about those things is in the *Ecclesiastical Constitutions*[154] of the Bishops in the year 1603, nor in the Anglican liturgy. Also there is no use of them in parish churches either outside or within the religious activities; so that this worship with the organ is wrongly attributed by some people to Anglican churches or the Anglican Church as a whole. The Oxonians in their own *Response*,[155] a humble petition of ministers in the year 1603, in which they ask *that the music for church singing be composed for better edification,* oppose nothing, nor do they defend a received practice at the time. But they seem to concede silently that moderation and reformation could be applied here; at the very least, they don't mention organs even once. Whatever might be the case concerning music and the organs remaining anywhere in England, I do not recall that they are appointed by their theologians to be a support, and indeed even a part, of divine worship in the same way as in the Old Testament; which Papist authors do, and Eckhard the Lutheran[156] in the work already cited; as we can clearly observe from their arguments, which will be refuted below. [Voetius adds: Maxwell, the Scottish theologian,[157] touches upon this matter in his vernacular tract about the superiority of the Anglican Church over the Genevan.] We on the contrary have established, with the Reformed theologians to be cited below, that organ music is neither an appropriate support, nor a part, nor an accessory of divine or ecclesiastical worship. [Voetius adds: Whatever may exist concerning its use or tolerance in various places which have preserved it thus far.]

IV. The direct arguments are the following [Voetius alters to: Our arguments are partly direct and partly indirect; the direct ones are these]. *Argument 1.* Because Christ and the apostles, or the apostolic church, did not use such music, nor did they teach the use of it in order to bring greater devotion or some sort of perfection to worship in church. Those who do use it, therefore, are tacitly suggesting that they are superior to the apostolic churches in wisdom, or zeal, or in a kind of fullness and happiness. *Argument 2.* Because it not only fails to excite, increase, and strengthen

---

be well vsed and abused also. Kneeling at the name of Iesus is of the lyke nature, ringing when matins is doone (as you tearme it) curious singing, organs, &c. All these be without the booke, and therfore without discretion alleged as a reason why you wil not subscribe to the book.

154. *Constitutions and canons ecclesiastical.*

155. "The Humble Petition" in *The Answere of.* A slightly modernized version may be found as "The Millenary Petition, 1603" in Kenyon, *Stuart Constitution*, 132–34.

156. In the 1663 text, Voetius omits Heimenbergius's *the Lutheran*.

157. Bishop John Maxwell (1590?–1647), the work could be *Episcopacie not abivred.*

the mind's spiritual and rational worship, but on the contrary it hinders, breaks, disperses, weakens, and enfeebles these things, while, through those perceptible things, it entices the powers and intention of the soul [or mind] away toward perceptible and inferior pleasures, and draws them away from the inward tasting of heavenly, divine, and unspeakable delight and joy (1 Peter 1:8 with 2:3). Thomas expresses this reasoning excellently, and together with him, Cajetan in 22 question 91 article 2: *Just as the Philosopher said in 8 Politic.,*[158] *neither should the reed pipes be brought into teaching situations, nor any other sort of professional instrument of music, for instance, the harp and anything else like that; but whatever things make them good listeners. For musical instruments of this kind move a soul more toward pleasure, rather than letting a good disposition be shaped by them.*[159] Argument 3. Even if it were a most excellent thing in itself, anything in public worship which neither edifies nor is suitable for edifying the church should not be used. But organ music is such a thing; therefore the major premise is proved from 1 Corinthians 14:12, 16, 17, 19, 26. The minor [premise] is proved, because while the organ is sounding either alone or antiphonally, the Church does not understand either the polyphonic modulation or the sacred words for which that modulation is called suitable, and consequently, she cannot say *Amen*. Please see 1 Corinthians 14: 7–11, 14, 16. Adversaries are compelled to admit this reasoning; just as the *Ceremoniale Episcoporum*, book I chapter 28, calls vocal music, as opposed to instrumental, obviously *intelligible: But when the Creed is said in Mass, the organ should not be intermingled, but it* [the Creed] *should be presented there by the choir with intelligible singing.* And a little before: *But attention will have to be paid, so that whenever something is designed for the organ, to be opposed or to be answered in alternation with versicles of hymns or canticles, whatever must be answered by the organ shall be pronounced by someone in the choir in an intelligible voice. And it would be commendable that some singer would sing the same in a clear voice, together with the organ.* Suarez, in volume 2 of *Concerning Religion*, treatise 4, book 4, chapter 8, chooses the same; and adds these reasons, *so that the integrity of the vocal prayer might be completed, for by the sound of instruments alone it does not seem to become a sufficiently vocal prayer, such as prayer in choir ought to be.* To the

---

158. *Politics* viii.6.

159. This last sentence is not from Aristotle's *Politics* viii.6, but from Saint Thomas's *Summa Theologiae*, Second Part of the Second Part, Question 91, Article 2, Reply to Objection 4.

wise doctor[160] the question from *Ceremoniale Episcoporum* just cited thus makes an exception: *When a verse is uttered by the organ alone, without any singing, it is customary for the choir to recite that verse without singing, which suffices indeed for the completeness of the Hour; but it does not seem so suitable for providing what is satisfactory to the people, and for public prayer. On the contrary, when this happens in the Creed, Navarrus, in n. 44 and 45 above, and more clearly in 49, judges that it is a sin. Argument 4.* Whatever is a fertile occasion of many evils, and liable to many abuses, should not be employed in public worship, if indeed it might be an indifferent thing,[161] or at least, in itself, might not be necessary or very useful; but such is the music of the organ; therefore it is better not to promote it in churches, since the spiritual damage and danger arising from it are greater than its usefulness. Experience approves the minor proposition, and reason does too; the Papist authors cited above (thesis 3) approve either of them well enough, especially Lindanus in *Panoply* and Cajetan in 22, question 91, article 2; compare Bellarmine in the work already cited, page 2686, and *Episcopale* p. 39 a. [Voetius adds here: Bochellus in the *Decisions of the French Church*, volume 1:7, chapters 23–31.][162]

V. [Voetius does not indicate a fifth paragraph here.] The indirect arguments are partly from the absurd conclusions, partly *ad hominem*. These are: *Argument 1.* Because it is redolent of Judaism, or the specific, immature, and ritualistic worship of the Old Testament; and by an equal right, the little bells of Aaron (Exodus 28:34–35), the silver trumpets of the priests (Numbers 10:2–3), the horns of Jubal (Leviticus 25:9), citharas, harps, cymbals, with the Levites singing (1 Chronicles 25: 1, 6), could be introduced into the New

---

160. σοφον φαρμακον. The phrase goes back to Euripides' *Phoenician Women*, lines 471–72:

ἔχει γὰρ αὐτὰ καιρόν: ὁ δ' ἄδικος λόγος
νοσῶν ἐν αὐτῷ φαρμάκων δεῖται σοφῶν.

In Euripides it appears to mean a "skillful medicine" or "a clever treatment." The phrase σοφον φαρμακον appears in several Reformation-era controversial works. Here it seems to mean a prudent and clever remedy in an ironical sense—something which is at best a cunning expedient and at worst quackery.

161. *adiaphorum*.

162. = Laurent Bouchel (1559–1629), *Decretorum Ecclesiae Gallicanae*, 82: *Crescente Ecclesia canendi & psallendi ritus publice, primum in Orientalibus, demum in Occidentalibus Ecclesiis, receptus est, & observatus: ad movendum & excitandum prasertim languentium & torpentium animorum affectum*. As the church grew, the practice of publicly singing and playing a stringed instrument was accepted and observed, first in the Eastern and finally in the Western churches, for the purpose of stirring and rousing the emotions, especially of listless and apathetic spirits.

Testament churches, and even universal ritualistic worship, or *the needy elements of the world*, as the apostle says at Galatians 4[:9]. And yet Thomas, in the place cited, rightly observes that this is absurd: *In the Old Testament the use of such instruments was employed, both because the people were more hardened and carnal—so that they needed to be aroused by instruments of this kind, just as also by earthly promises—and because physical instruments of this kind were figures of something else.* We will refute exceptions to this argument below. *Argument 2.* Because it is a gentile affectation[163] and is proper for their worship; which is absurd. For as the gentiles used to mingle games and shows with their solemn festivals and sacred rites, they also did so with music. Thus Ctesibius dedicated his own water-vessel[164] which played both warlike and joyful and festive tunes by the rushing of water in the temple of Zephyr (also known as Venus Arsinoe), [Voetius omits: about which Hedylus wrote his *Epigrams*]. The witness is Lactantius book 2, chapter 7: *Heathens are wont to come to the temples, not so much for the sake of religion, as so that they may see what may entertain them.* Concerning theatrical music and religious rites of our ancestors, see Boulenger *On the Theater*, book 2. [Voetius alters to: See Boulenger, *On the Theater*, book 2, chapter 31, concerning the inventors of the hydraulis, and the same author, *On the Theatrical Music of the Ancients*, from chapter 2, etc.[165]] *Argument 3.* It would follow that also many other things, which the senses can perceive, and which are carnal, should be introduced into public worship, for the sake of some carnal or ignorant people who are affected by these things; dancing (of course), theater, games, and any delights whatsoever of the ears and eyes: but this is absurd. But let an exception be made: we wish nothing to be received, except what is decorous, or what was formerly used commonly in the Old Testament. I respond: why therefore are the bells, trumpets, cymbals, citharas [lyres], pipes, and music of David not introduced along with the dancing and the dancers of the Israelites (Exodus 15 etc.)? From that point, will they

---

163. κακοζηλία.

164. ρυτόν. A rhyton normally means a water vessel for pouring. It apparently used a stream of water to power some type of mechanism that played a tune. But this is not the same as a hydraulis, which was played at will by a human being. Ctesibius was an engineer, credited with other inventions besides the hydraulis. The temple was not dedicated to Zephyr, god of the west wind, but to Queen Arsinoe II of Egypt, whose cult was associated with Aphrodite/Venus, as Voetius correctly states. Because of the name of the temple's location, Cape Zephyrion, she came to be associated with Zephyr, but he was not the primary focus of the cult.

165. Voetius places this alteration before the citation of Lactantius, in place of the mention of Hedylus's *Epigrams*.

approve of those instruments and those rites which are more indecorous than their organs and the brass wind instruments which are often added to the organs? *Argument 4.* It would follow that the Church, both the apostolic one and the ancient one throughout so many centuries, was less devout, or at least less attentive to stirring up the devotion of their listeners, especially of the more ignorant and weaker sort: things which the Papists themselves confess [Voetius adds: or are forced to confess] are all absurd, as do other admirers of antiquity, who elsewhere wish that all our holy acts of worship be examined and recalled to the modest measure of the ancient Church. *Argument 5.* It would follow that the public or ecclesiastical exercises of piety (among which is doxology, or praise of God through psalms and hymns) are able to take place apart from the Church, and to be restricted to some definite people specially assigned and consecrated for that purpose: obviously, organists and the wind instrument players currently associated with them, and musicians or choir boys. But these things are absurd, and contradictory to Ephesians 5:19, Colossians 3:15–17, and to the practice of the primitive Church, in the writings of Tertullian[166] in *Apology* chapter 2, the letters of Pliny the Younger,[167] Justin[168] in the second *Apology*, Basil in letter 63,[169] Chrysostom's *Homily 1* on Isaiah chapter 8.[170] Baronius[171] also acknowledges

---

166. = Quintus Septimius Florens Tertullianus (145–220).

167. = Gauis Plinius Caecilius Secundus (61–113).

168. = Justin Martyr (100–165), *Divi Ivstini*, 317: *Quaestio 107: Si ab infidelibus ad imposturam inuenta sunt carmina, & in lege introducta sunt propter animi puerilitatem, cur qui gratiae perfectam & ab illis modis alienam disciplinam acceperunt, carminibus utuntur in ecclesiis more puerorum legis? Responsio: Non canere simpliciter est pueris conuéniens: sed cum inanimis instrumentis canere, & cum saltatione & crepitaculis. Itaque in ecclesiis sublatus est ex carminibus usus talium instrumentorum, & aliorum pueris conuenientium, & relictum est canere simpliciter. Excitat enim haec res animum ad ardentem cupiditatem eius quod in carminibus canitur: sopit insurgentes ex carne affectiones: cogitationes malas expellit, quae nobis ab inuisibilibus inimicis inijciuntur: irrigat animam ad ferendos fructus diuinorum bonorum: generosos reddit ad rerum aduersarum tolerantiam certatores pietatis, & omnium quae in uita accidunt rerum tristium remedium affert pijs. Paulus quidem gladium spiritus hoc nominat, ubi contra inuisibiles hostes armat milites pietatis. Est enim uerbum dei quod dum cogitatur & canitur & pulsatur, fugat daemones perficientia animam in uirtutibus pietatis, dum pijs contingunt per ecclesiastica carmina.*

169. = Caesariensis Basilius (330–379), *Divi Basilii*, 689.

170. Chrysostom's commentary on Isaiah was published in Greek for the first time by Henry Savile. Savile's Greek was then (re)published by Fronton du Duc with an added Latin translation by Carthusian monk Gottfriend Tilmann in 1609: *Sancti Patris nostri Ioannis*. For *Isaiah* homilies, see 3:640–767.

171. = Caesar Baronius (1538–1607), *Annales Ecclesiastici*, year 60:28: *Illud autem*

and shows from antiquity, in [*Annales Ecclesiastici*] Year 60 Section 28, that formerly the people also sang together indiscriminately with the clergy in church; however, an alteration was finally made, in canon 15 of the Council of Laodicea.[172] *Argument 6.* It would follow, that because of carnal and more ignorant people, the universal Church would be deprived, for such a great span of time, of the most noble and most excellent method for leading people to God, which is through preaching, reading, prayer, intelligible and shared psalmody. But it is absurd for precious hours of public gatherings to be wasted by these [other] things, and for souls to be sent out starving on nothing but bran, or inflated by bellows and wind, instead of having been fed; we have heard above, from Erasmus, that this was maintained in the papacy. *Calling people to devotion by teaching and preaching is a more excellent way than by singing,* says Thomas, already cited. What would he have said about the sound of organs, if indeed he had heard it in churches then?

VI. [Voetius does not indicate a sixth paragraph here.] Let the indirect arguments,[173] or ad hominem be these. *Argument 1.* That such ornamentation and highly varied[174] instrumental music are inimical to simplicity, spiritual inwardness, retreat, and the nakedness of the mind, and being uplifted away from external and corporeal things; which they commend so greatly to the devout, in the treatise *Concerning Contemplation and Mystical Theology*, with which we have dealt in the *Disputation Concerning*

---

non prætermittimus dicere de usu priston, olim promiscue una cum clericis in Ecclesia cantasse et populum, simuluque sacerdoti orationem danti vel colligenti responsere consuevisse. Ad hæc spectat illud S. Hieronymi Ad similitudinem cælestis tonitrui, Amen reboat; *et illu Ausonii in Ephemeride:* Consona quem celebrant modulati carmina David, / Et responsuris ferit aera vocibus, Amen. *Verum quoniam imperitia canentium sæpius accidebat, ut harmonicam illam ecclesiasticædignitati congreuentem cantionem incomposito vocum sono corrumperent, in quos (ut superius dictum est) Joannes Chrysostomus jure decclamat: ideireo necessario ecclesiasticis institutis provisum est, ne præter certos ad hoc opus adscriptos quis in ecclesia psalleret. Canon enim Laodiceni Concilii id prohibens ait:* Non licere præter canonicos psaltes, id est, qui regulariter cantores existent, quique pulpitum ascendant, et de codice legunt, alium quemlibet in ecclesia psallere.

172. *Laod. 15.* Περὶ τῶν ἐν ἄμβωνι ψάλλειν ὀφειλόντων. Περί τού μὴ δεῖν πλήν τῶν κανονικῶν ἐπί τόν ἄμβωνά ἀναβαινόντων καί ἀπό διφθέρας ψαλλόντων, ἑτέρους τινάς ψάλλειν ἐν ἐκκλησίᾳ. De his qui debeant in ambone, id est in pulpito, psallere. Quod non oporteat amplius praeter eos, qui regulariter cantores existunt, qui et de codice canunt, alios in pulpitum conscendere. Who shall sing on the platform. Apart from the canonical singers, who go up onto the platform and sing from parchments, no others shall sing in the church. *Discipline générale,* IX:I:2, 136.

173. κατ ἄνθρωπον.

174. πολυποικιλία.

Meditation and *Concerning Devotion*. Argument 2. It is opposed to simplicity, and to the cautious moderation of the ancient Church in making use of vocal and intelligible song: which was so great, that even in the time of Bishop Augustine there were Westerners who permitted no singing, as Alberto Pio recognizes in the place cited above. And indeed it is established, by Augustine's *Confessions*, book 9 chapter 7, that it [singing] was accepted late by the Western churches, and was first introduced on a particular occasion by Ambrose of Milan.[175] Argument 3. Singing [i.e., modern singing] is opposed to simplicity; for the ancients, as much as the Catholics themselves, did not want singing to be ornamented by the division [of notes] or by the harmonic multiplication of voices, and people to be led astray from attentiveness in such a way; and even less did they want them to be confused and separated from recollection and direction of the mind, by that difficult harmony of organs. The singing of the ancients consisted of a certain distinct and gravely measured delivery, from which excessive inflections of voices and consonance were absent. Athanasius, with the approval of Augustine in the place cited, ordered the lector to inflect his voice so moderately that he should represent someone reading aloud rather than singing.[176] Likewise, in [the *Confessions*] book 10 chapter 33: *When it happens to me that a song moves me more than the thing about which it is sung, I confess that I have committed a sin deserving punishment, and then I would prefer not to listen to someone singing.*[177] Bernard does the same in *Meditations* chapter 11,[178] and Jerome on Ephesians 5:19 where he says, *that the throat and jaws should not be soothed with medicine, as is the custom for tragedies, in order that theater-style measures and songs might be heard in church.*[179] See and compare canon 75 of the Sixth Council of Constantinople

---

175. = Ambrosius Mediolanensis (339–397). Augustine recounts a siege on Palm Sunday 386 when soldiers surrounded Ambrose's church. Ambrose and his congregation sheltered inside for several days, strengthening themselves by singing: *Tunc hymni et psalmi ut canerentur secundum morem orientalium partium, ne populus maeroris taedio contabescerent, institutum est: ex illo in hodiernum retentum multis iam ac paene omnibus gregibus tuis et per cetera orbis imitantibus.* Augustine, *Augustinus*, 446.

176. See Migne, *Patrologiae Cursus Completus*, 28:331.

177. *tamen cum mihi accidit, ut me amplius cantus quam res, quae canitur, moveat, poenaliter me peccare confiteor, et tunc mallem non audire cantantem.* Nicene and Post-Nicene Fathers, I:50.

178. Bernard of Clairvaux (1090–1153), *Meditationes de interiori homine*, 25ff.

179. = Sophronius Eusebius Hieronymus (Jerome, 347–420), *Sancti Eusebii Hieronymi*, col. 528f: *Qui se abstinuerit ab ebrietate vini, in quo est luxuria, et pro hoc spiritu fuerit impletus, iste omnia potest accipere spiritualiter, psalmos, hymnos, et cantica. Quid autem*

in Trullo,[180] and Denis the Carthusian's[181] treatise *Concerning the Life of Priests*, article 20, where in the divine office he prohibits a breaking up of the vocal sound, and singing of a highest part:[182] *Although, he says, the highest voice part may especially arouse certain people to devotion and contemplation of heavenly things, nevertheless it often seems to draw back and to prevent the senses from being attentive, even to one's own prayer which one is hearing and praying.*[183] Anonymous's *Summa of Virtues and Vices* (and cited

---

intersit inter psalmum et hymnum et canticum, in Psalterio plenissime discimus. Nunc autem breviter hymnos esse dicendum, qui fortitudinem et majestatem prædicant Dei, et ejusdem semper, vel beneficia, vel facta mirantur. Quod omnes psalmi continent, quibus Alleluia, vel præpositum, vel subjectum est, psalmi autem proprie ad ethicum locum pertinent, ut per organum corporis, quid faciendum, et quid vitandum sit, noverimus. Qui vero de superioribus disputat, et concentum mundi omniumque creaturarum ordinem atque concordiam subtilis disputator edisserit, ise spirituale canticum canit. Vel certe (ut propter simpliciores manifestius quod volumus, eloquamur) psalmus ad corpus: canticum refertur ad mentem. Et canere igitur et psallere, et laudare Dominum magis animo quam voce debemus. Hoc est quippe quod dicitur: Cantantes et psallentes in cordibus vestris Domino. Audiant haec adolescentuli: audiant hi quibus psallendi in ecclesia officium est, Deo non voce, sed corde cantandum: nec in tragoedorum modum guttur et fauces dulci medicamine colliniendas, ut in ecclesia theatris moduli audiantur et cantica, sed in timore, in opere, in scientia Scripturarum. Quamvis sit aliquis ut solent illi appealellare κακόφωνος, si bona opera habuerit, dulcis apud Deum cantor est. Sic cantet servus Christi, ut non vox canentis, sed verba placeant quae leguntur: ut spiritus malus qui erat in Saule I Reg populorum.

180. Also called the Quinisext Council, held in 692. The text of the canon reads: LXXV. Περὶ τοῦ μὴ βοαῖς ἀτάκτοις ἐν τῷ ψάλλειν κεχρῆσθαι. Τοὺς ἐπὶ τὸ ψάλλειν ἐν ταῖς ἐκκλησίας παραγινομένους βουλόμεθα μήτε βοαῖς ἀτάκτοις κεχρῆσθαι καὶ τὴν φύσιν πρὸς κραυγὴν ἐκβιάξεσθαι, μήτε τι ἐπιλέγειν τῶν μὴ τῇ ἐκκλμσίᾳ ἁρμοδίων τε καὶ οἰκείων· ἀλλὰ μετὰ πολλῆς πποσοχῆς τε καὶ κατανύξεως τὰς τοιαύτας ψαλμῳδίας προσάγειν τῷ τῶν κρυπτῶν ἐφόρῳ θεῷ. ʽεὐλαβεῖς γρὰ ἔσεθσαι τύος Ἰσραήλʼ, τὸ ἱερὸν ἐδίδαξε λόγιον. *Discipline générale* IX:I:1, 212. = *Eos qui in ecclesiis ad psallendum accedunt, volumus nec inordinatis vociferationibus uti, & naturam ad clamorem urgere; nec aliquid eorum, quae ecclesia non convenient, & apta non sunt, afcifcere; sed cum magna attentione & compunction psalmodies Deo, qui est occultorum inspector, offerre. Pios enim & sanctos fore silio Israel, sacrum docuit oraculum. Sacrosancta Concilia*, 1176. We want them who have become singers in the churches not to use unruly shouting nor to force nature to scream or add anything to what is considered appropriate in the church, but with great care and piety to offer the hymns to God, the one who sees the secrets. For the holy Word has taught the children of Israel to be pious.

181. = Dionysius Carthusian (1402–1471).

182. *discantus.*

183. Carthusianus, *Vita sacerdotum*, 54: *De vita canonicorum*, art.20: . . . *quidam qui ad tempus sic cantare consueverunt, fatentur superbiam et quamdam lasciviam animi in hujuscemodi cantu consistere. Porro, si aliquo modo debeat excusari, non videtur excusabilis aut commendabilis esse nisi pro devotione excitanda ordinetur ac fiat. Nam quidam ex melodiis ad contemplationem et devotionem fortiter excitantur: unde et organa habet*

in the same place by the Carthusian) says: *Just as the wind usually causes rippling in the water, so the wind of vanity usually causes this rippling and breaking of the voice.*[184] John XXII[185] in the *Extravagantes Communes*, book 3 title 1, censures singers in worship who *break up chant*[186] *melodies with hockets*[187] *and make them slippery with descants, frequently inserting second and third voices in the vernacular, etc.*[188] All of which he prohibits severely, making a concession to the torrent of use, or of abuse, by means of the clause alone: *However, by this we do not intend to prohibit* [harmonies], *but rather, sometimes on feast days, etc.* . . . *let some harmonies which resemble the melody, namely the octaves, fifths, fourths, and the like, be presented above the simple ecclesiastical chant, yet in a way that the integrity of the chant itself may remain unimpaired, etc.*[189] Alberto Pio in the place cited

---

Ecclesia. Si vero fiat ad oblectandum praesentibus, etiam mulieribus, non dubium quin reprehensibile exstet . . . Denique, quamvis discantus provocet specialiter quosdam ad devotionem et contemplationem coelestium, multum tamen revocare videtur ac impedire ab advertentia sensus etiam propriae orationis ejus qui audit et orat.

184. = Guillelmus Peraldus (1190–1271), *Summae de vitiis*, ii: 288: *Et sicut ventus solet facere in aqua crispationem quandam: sic ventus vanitatis hanc crispationem seu fractionem vocis frequenter facit.* Carthusian's quote (54): . . . *sicut ventus facere solet crispationem in aqua, sic ventus vanitatis hanc crispationem fractionemque voci facere solet.*

185. Pope John XXII (note that Heimenbergius omits his title, perhaps intentionally) lived from 1244 to 1334. Hocketing (see footnote below) was practiced in the music of his time.

186. Voetius deletes "chant."

187. Voetius changed Heimenbergius' *hoquetis* to *loquetis*, perhaps because hocketing was no longer known nor used. *Hocketing* was a technique found in polyphonic music starting in the thirteenth century. In its simplest form it is the rapid alternation of rests and notes between two or more voices. When one voices pauses, the other sings, giving the effect of gasps or hiccups. In addition, some medieval composers added hocketing with one singer; in that case, the melody was not sung in normal phrases but in short phrases alternated quickly with rests. Pope John XXII's *Docta sanctorum* of 1324 criticized hocketing and, as mentioned in the text, discant, and French motets. See *Corpus juris canonici* 2:256.

188. *Corpus iuris canonici*, cols. 1255–7: *Nam melodias hoquetis intersecant, discantibus lubricant, triplis et motetis vulgaribus nonnunquam inculcant. discantibus lubricant, triplis & motetis vulgaribus nonnumquam inculcant, &c.* A medieval motet had a tenor part, a sustained part used as a foundation, with or without text. Additional voices added above the tenor were labeled by their proximity to the tenor: "duplum" or "motetus" ("second voice" or "part with words"), "triplum" (third voice, next nearest), quadruplum (= fourth voice), etc. Discantus was used to indicate the highest voice. Often each part above the tenor had a completely different text, frequently vernacular or secular. Clearly, as medieval theorists point out, this music was linguistically confusing.

189. *Corpus iuris canonici.* cols. 1324–5: *Per hoc autem non intendimus prohibere,*

above rejects every polyphonic[190] song, or "musical" song. [Voetius adds: Filesac,[191] in *Selectorum liber secundus*, in the title *Concerning Church Singing*, sections 12–13, mentions turns,[192] and sweet voices capable of division and clashing.] *Argument 4*. Because other musical instruments should not be used in church; as the *Ceremoniale Episocoporum* decrees in book 1, chapter 23, and Bellarmine warns in chapter 17 (cited) page 2686, and Suarez in the place cited (however much he may waffle in the discourse and contradict himself in his customary way). Therefore, by analogy, neither organs nor yet difficult organ music [are used]. Rather, if anything is to be tolerated, the simpler instruments like brass horns, trumpets, lyres, citharas, and so on, can be tolerated with greater right. And the arguments of the Papists, drawn from the example of the Old Testament, and from the practice of devotion and the praise of God, are equally binding for these as for the organs. *Argument 5*. Because they [the Papists] do not adhere to the practice of venerable antiquity. For they pretend everywhere that they still especially aspire to it, but obviously in this respect they prefer the novelties of the Greeks to the ancient and weighty devotion. [Voetius adds: For, *firstly*, they cannot deny that the invention of the organ is recent.] Jules-César Boulenger, in *On the Theater*, book 2, chapter 31, refers to the times of Julian the Apostate.[193] Lorinus in his *Commentary on the book of Wisdom*, 19:17 (in Greek ψαλτήριον),[194] and Polydore Vergil, book 3, chapter 7, refuse to agree about the inventor. There are those who attribute it [i.e. the invention of the organ] to Gerbert of Aurillac [Voetius adds: or

---

quin interdum diebus fetis praecique, sive solennibus in missis et praefatis divinis officiis aliquae consonantiae, quae melodiam sapient, puta octavae, quintae, quartae et huiusmodi supra cantum ecclesiasticum simplicem proferantur, sic tamen, ut ipsius cantus integritas illibata permaneat. Pope John XXII is suggesting "parallel organum," i.e. harmony at the fourth, fifth, or octave, moving in the same intervals as the chant melody.

190. πολίφωνον.

191. = Jean Filesac (1550–1638), *Ionnis Filesaci Selectorum*, 214–17.

192. *flexuras*.

193. Flavius Claudius Julianus, grandson of Constantine (331–363), *Juliani Imp[eratori] Opera*, 01r: *Quam cerno, alterius naturae est fistula: nempe Altera produxit fortasse hanc aenea tellus: Horrendum stridet, nec nostris illa movetur Flatibus, at missus taurino è carcere ventus. Subtus agit leves calamos, pérque ima vagatur. Mox aliquis velox digitiis, insignis & arte Adstat, concordes calamis pulsátque tabellas: Ast illæ subito exiliunt, & carmina miscent.*

194. The phrase in parentheses is in Heimenbergius, but Voetius moved it later in the text: "The text of Wisdom 19:17 in Greek contains the word ψαλτήριον. The Vulgate text has 'organo.'"

1 | PROFESSORS

Sylvester II[195]], others to [Voetius adds: the priest] George of Venice, still others to more ancient people (as Polydore says the same, op. cit., and Genebrard[196] in his *Chronographia*), but these are pure conjectures. Whatever it may be, this invention must be attributed to the Greeks or Asians, since not only does their ingenuity make us believe this, but also the *Annals of the Franks*[197] concerning the deeds of Pepin, and Aventinus, in the *History of Bavaria*, book 3, [Voetius adds: and Marianus Scotus,] which mention that an organ was sent as a gift by Constantine Copronymus[198] through legates, as though it were a wondrous and rare thing; and Baronius acknowledges this history in section 21 on the year 766, and before him, Genebrard in the *Chronographia* for the year 715,[199] who adds that "up to that time those organs had been unknown to the Franks and the Germans." [Voetius moves the following citation and adds: and Molanus de Canonicis lib. 2. C. 40.] Aimonius, in the *History of the Franks*, book 4, chapter 113, also mentions that a certain Greek priest named George[200] had built an

---

195. Praetorius says, 145, that Gerbert, bishop of Rheims, who was later named Pope Sylvester II (946–1003), constructed an organ which produced musical tones by the power of heated water in 997. Zwinger says, in *Theatrum Humanæ*, 3714: *Georgivs sacerdos Venetiis oriundus, à Baldrico comite Pannoniæ Ludouico Pio commendatus, musicæ hydranticum instrumentum, quod Organon uocant, ad Aquas Graneas conflauit. Aimonius lib. 4. Cap. 113. de Francis, Auentinus lib. 4. Annalium.*

196. = Gilbert Génébrard (1535–1597), *Gilb. Genebrardi theologi Parisiensis*, 3:512: *An. 757. Constantinus Pipino organa musica misit, hactenus Germani & Gallis incognita. Aventinus lib.3. Annalium. Marianus Scotus. Anon. de Gestia Francorum lib. 4. cap. 64.*

197. The Franks' *Annales regni Francorum* were transmitted in two different versions: the *Annales Laurissenses Maiores* and the *Annales Einhardi*. The records of both from *Annales Regni Francorum inde ab a. 741. usque ad a. 829*, Kurze and Pertz, eds. (Hannover: Hahniani, 1895), 15: from *Annales Laurissenses: 757. Misit Constantinus imperator regi Pippino cum a/iis donis organum, qui in Franciam usque pervenit. Et rex Pippinus tenuit placitum suum in Conpendio [sic] cum Francis, ibique Tassilo venit, dux Baioariorum, in vasatico se commendans per manus, sacramenta iuravit multa et innumerabilia, reliquias sanctorum martyrum manus inponens [sic], et fidelitatem promisit regi Pippino et supradictis filiis eius, domno Carlomanno.* From *Annales Einhardi: 757. Constantinus imperator misit Pippino regi multa munera, inter quae et organum; quae ad eum in Conpendio [sic] villa pervenerunt, ubi tunc populi sui generalem conventum habuit.Illuc et Tassilo dux Baioariorum cum primoribus gentis suae venit, et more Francico in manus regis in vassaticum manibus suis semetipsum commen-davit, fidelitatemque tam ipso regi Pippino quam filiis eius Karlo et Karlomanno iureiurando supra corpus sancti Dionisii promisit.*

198. = Constantine V Copronymus (718–775).

199. The year is incorrect. It is probably meant to be 757, for Pepin ruled 751–768, and Constantine 741–775.

200. Voetius refers not to Gregorium, but to a "L. Georgium," likely George of Venice

organ after the Greek fashion for the Emperor Louis. [Voetius adds: Lorinus, in the place already cited [*Commentary on*] *the book of Wisdom, 19:17*, acknowledges that the word *organum* (Greek ψαλτήριον) is usable for every kind of musical instrument; *later, especially in popular speech, it was used for a particular one to which bellows were attached; and Isidore refers the reason for this name to a popular* (note this!) *custom of the Greeks.*[201] In the same place he cites Augustine [in the *Exposition*] on *Psalm* 56, and Amalarius, *De ecclesiasticis officiis*, book 3, chapter 8.[202] Concerning the newness of the organ, compare Hospinian[203] *De templis*, book 2, chapter 23, and *Historia sacra*[*mentaria*], part 1, book 3, chapter 3. Among the Lutherans, Micraelius[204] in his *Syntagma historiarum Ecclesiae*, page 547, confesses his doubt about their antiquity. *Secondly*, we find that the lack of use of an organ in churches was accepted everywhere, except after the time of Thomas Aquinas, who flourished in the year 1270. And Cajetan and Navarrus support us in the place cited, and the latter in the book *On Hours and Prayer*, chapters 16, 17; as also George of Venice on the 22nd question 91, article 2. On behalf of slightly more ancient antiquity, Johannes Stephanus [Voetius adds: Durantus[205]] opposes them (*On the Rites of the Church*, loc.

---

as confirmed by Aimonius IV:113 and Aventinus III:294.

201. Lorinus, 703: . . . *deinde, juxta vulgi praesertim sermonem, ad certu, eui folles adhibentur, & cuius nominis rationem Isidorus refert ad vulgarem consuetudinem Graecorum.*

202. = Amalarius of Metz (Amalarius Fortunatus Trevirensis, 775–853), *Amalarii Epsicopi Opera Liturgica*, I:III:8:268: *Unde Agustinus in libro Psalmorum novissimi psalmi: Idem ipsi sancti sunt in omnibus musicis organis. Et Paulo post: Laudate Dominum in sanctis eius. Hoc exsequitur varie, significans eosdem ipsos sanctos eius; Laudate eum in sono tubae, propter laudis excelsissimam claritatem . . .*

203. = Rudolf Hospinian (Rudolf Wirth, 1547–1626).

204. = Johannes Micraelius (Johannes Lütkeschwager, 1597–1658), *Syntagma historiarum Ecclesiae*, 246–47: *Quae tamen utrum concinnis & artificiosis notris organis conformia suerint, dubitamus. Haec enim aliqui a Theophilo Imperatore esse inventa, aliqui vetustiora esse; aliqui autorem eorum prorsus ignorari, dicunt. A Vitaliano Papa circa A.C. DCLX. ea in templis recepta, & per consonantias humanis vocibus adhibita fuisse, testature Balaeus: In Galliam tempore Pipini A.C. DCCLVII. dono Constantini Imperatoris transportata esse, autor est Aventinuae in annalibus Bojorum, & Marianus Scotus in Chronicis. Bernhardum vero Teutonem circa A.C. MCDLXXX, auxisse numeros, &, ut pedes quoque; attractu suniculorum concentum juvarent, fecisse, dicit Sabellicus enn. X. lib. viii. Hospinainus lib II. de templis cap. XXIII. Addit, eum in fabricandis organis luxum coepisse adhiberi, ut Michael, Constantinopolitanus Imperator, ea ex auro confiari, & abbas quidam Salernitanus fistulam in longitudine XXVIII. pedum, & in circumferential IV. spithamarum fieri curaverit.*

205. Voetius adds *Durantus* to clarify: The first Durant mentioned in this sentence

1 | PROFESSORS

cit.) and with him Suarez and Molanus in book 2 chapter 40 of *De canonicis*, in the place cited, mentioning [Guillaume] Durant in his *Rationale*, book 4, chapter 34, who was a contemporary of Thomas [Aquinas]. But the answer is that at the time of Thomas Aquinas, and perhaps before that, there was some use of these things, but only in the chapels of kings and important people, or in certain cathedral churches, in just the same way that comedies have been exhibited in churches somewhere, and other worldly rubbish of this nature; still, this use is not common in the churches, not to speak of it being ecclesiastically or generally prescribed or accepted. This Molanus clearly confesses, in chapter 40, and it is satisfactorily concluded from the *Extravagantes* of John XXII, just cited. Moreover, it serves as an argument, that in the presence of the Roman Pope the church never makes use of this (as witnessed by Cajetan, Navarrus, Molanus): as Molanus says, *as an indication that their use in the Church is new, or at least not altogether ancient.* In the cathedral church of Liège (where Molanus published his treatise, *De Canonicis*) up to the year 1585, they had music alternately, or from both sides, and without the ordinary use of organs at different places.[206] There is another opinion that is held by the champions of the antiquity of organs: that their use began at the time of Pope Vitalian in the year 606, and after the year 820 in the time of King Louis the Pious. I answer that these are sheer conjectures, as you will learn from Molanus: *However,* he says, *I believe that the most Christian princes* (Louis and the Kings of France) *soon brought the organs, which until then had been unused among them and for which they gave thanks to God, for the use in church services, following the example of the holy fathers*[207] (that is, David and Solomon, as he soon explains with Durant). You see now an outstanding demonstration of its antiquity and catholicity. The first origin of the instruments in the West was from Constantine Copronymus and a Greek priest (see, in

---

is Johannes Stephanus Durant (= Jean-Etienne Durand, 1534–1589) who wrote the *De ritibus Ecclesiae Catholicae libri tres* (1594); and the second Durant referenced is Guillaume Durant de St-Pourcain (1275–1334), bishop of Meaux, who wrote the *Rationale divinorum officiorum*, and was a contemporary of Aquinas.

206. The Cathedral of our Lady of Antwerp. During the Iconoclasm of August 20, 1566, at the start of the Eighty Years' War, Protestants destroyed a large part of the cathedral interior. Later, when Antwerp came under Protestant administration in 1581, a number of artistic treasures were once again destroyed, removed, or sold. The restoration of Roman Catholic authority came in 1585 with the fall of Antwerp.

207. Johannes Molani, *De Canonicis*, 215.

the *Annales* of Baronius, how pleasing the name Copronymus[208] was to the popes!), and so this was the occasion of their use in church. But their use spread out late from the kings of France (I believe it was in their courts, and afterward in the private chapels of their courts, and so on, one after another.) This, doubtless, is the authority and the good order[209] of the laws and of church worship! Platina (from whom Baptista Mantuanus and Balteus [Voetius alters to Baleus] get it) understands this to be about Vitalian; but I think it is established by his [Platina's] words alone what faith should be placed in his account, unless by chance one would grant that he [Vitalian] (as an eminent musician indeed) took care of such an organ for himself, for private use and enjoyment. Here we see by what right Bayllius the Jesuit proclaims in his *Catechesis* (loc. cit. above): that *its use is most ancient. Thirdly,* that ornamented or artistic singing indeed began somewhere in the West around the year 735, as Daneus[210] observes (in *Isagoges Christianae,* part 4, book 4, chapter 22). And I believe that it is established from the *Extravagantes* of John XXII, and the *Summa Virtutum,* and Denis the Carthusian, cited above, that this certainly had dared to exist as a private and disorderly[211] arrangement, not as a common and ecclesiastical good order.[212] To these Molanus is unable to respond in any way in his *De Canonicis,* book 2, chapter 39, except for this: *But if the singing may be understood through the descant and the ornamentation by the voice, and the modulation is according to the art of music, to wish to condemn these is to depart from common sense, and from the opinion of the Church. Thus the Council of Trent, etc.*

VII. [Voetius does not indicate a seventh paragraph here.] But with respect to these arguments of ours, we add on the authorities and consensus, first, of the ancients; second, of the medieval period (sometimes better, sometimes extremely corrupt), up to the time of the Reformation; third, of churches and teachers now, forward from the time of the Reformation, of whom some are Papist, and some our people. 1. Universal practice has taught us tacitly what the consensus of the ancient church was that their

---

208. = "dung name," because Copronymus allegedly defecated during his baptism.

209. εὐταξία.

210. = Lambert Daneau (1530–1595), *Isagoges Christianae,* published in at least five parts. Voetius's 1663 edition gives a citation which may have been incomplete or incorrect in Heimenbergius's original.

211. ἄτακτα.

212. Τάξιν, see 1 Corinthians 14:40.

worship was without organ music; and that the church fathers never force upon them devotion with an organ, in relation to Psalm 33 or 150, or 1 Corinthians 14 and similar texts, where at least there was an opportunity, if anywhere. And with regard to their moral and ascetic practices, where they commend prayers, hymns, and psalm-singing, there is profound silence about this devotion; finally that they banish these things to the peculiar and instructional worship of the Old Testament, like the author of the *Questions* under the name of Justin [Martyr] (question 107), and Chrysostom on 1 Corinthians 14, and Augustine's *De civ[itate] Dei*, book 17, chapter 14. We will not refute the exceptions of our adversaries, because they are willingly putting their hands to the task (Bellarmine, Molanus, Cajetan, Navarrus, Valentia, in the places cited), and they recognize the novelty. Bellarminus's petty exception cannot remove the saying of Clement in the *Paedagogus*, book 2, chapter 4,[213] from the testimony that has to be stated; for although Clement had spoken there about the use of instruments at feasts among Christians, he still could not prohibit or limit that use, unless he were to accept it as sacred. In so doing he would have equally satisfied both gentiles and Christians.[214] [Voetius does not include the next sentence:] But the printer and the time are warning me to break this off.

SUMMARIES

I. Whether public singing in church assemblies is a thing permitted and indifferent, or illicit by being forbidden, or an obligation? A. pr.[215]

213. Clement of Alexandria (= Titus Flavius Clemens, 150-215), *Clementis Alexandrini*, IV:53: *Divinum autem ministerium separans psallit spiritus: Laudate eum in sono tubae. In sono enim tubae suscitabit mortuos: Laudate eum in psalterio, quoniam lingua est psalterium Domini. Et in cithara laudate eum. Per citharam os intelligatur, quod spiritu tanquam plectro pulsatur. In tympano & choro laudate eum. Dicit Ecclesiam quem meditata est carnis resurrectionem in pelle resonante. In chordis & organo laudate eum. Organum dicit corpus nostrum, & chordas eius nervos, per quos numerosè & concinnè intenditur, & spiritu pulsatum, voces edit humanas. Laudate eum in cymbalis iubilationis. Oris cymbalum dicit linguam, quae pulsatis labris resonat. Et ideo humanae naturae acclamauit: Omnis spiritus laudet Dominum: quoniam omnis spiritus quem fecit, curam gessit. Verè enim pacificum instrumentum homo est.*

214. At this point Heimenbergius brings the first part of his thesis defense to an end. Voetius in his 1663 edition (559, line 4ff.) omits Heimenbergius's list of summaries, and continues section 7, jumping to the beginning of Heimenbergius's text in Part 2 of his thesis, without any indication of a break.

215. Affirmative.

II. Whether it is appropriate for public song to be in harmony and ornamented? N.[216]

III. Whether organ music should be retained in church worship, or introduced anew? N.

IV. Whether it is consistent with the Reformation to introduce organs into churches anew and to do this for the incitement of devotion in those who are about to sing, or for the direction of the signing, or for bringing splendor and grace together in a sacred activities? N.

V. Whether organists, in this respect, are ecclesiastical assistant—at least secondary ones, like lectors and music leaders—especially if they are Papists, and are unable to pray and to make music with our church with one mind and spirit, on account of the strength of their religious belief? N.

VI. Whether and in what way the common and official use of organs or other instruments in churches (Protestant churches) as well as in homes and in public and common gathering places can be maintained. Disq.[217]

VII. Whether such an official use of organs is more tolerable and less dangerous outside church worship and gathering, than that other practice in gathering and worship? A. pr.

VIII. Whether by the private authority of magistrates, or of one or another official person, or perhaps by one or another minister shutting his eyes to is, the ancient use of organs in public worship, or some part of it, namely in singing, may and ought to be introduced safely and in a seemly manner? N.

IX. Whether, against approved and long-standing practice, nay also against the ecclesiastical constitutions of our churches, as also against the teaching of the first reformers in The Netherlands[218]—in one church, independently from the rest, a change can take place in this practice, without the earlier judgment of other churchmen in classical and synodical correspondence? N.

The End

216. No.
217. Discussed, and disputed.
218. *Belgio.*

GISBERTUS VOETIUS

Appendix Apologetica (1663)

Gisbertus Voetii, *Politicæ Ecclesiasticæ*, Tract II. De Precib., Benedict., Doxolog. Eccl. Cap. III. Fol. 592:

Appendix Apologetica

In the year 1634, in the month of August, among other questions which were going to be aired in the first disputation at the beginning of my professorship in the Gymnasium of Utrecht, I had proposed this also: "that organ music is neither a part of nor a supplement to public worship." In a certain little book entitled *An Examination of the First Disputation*,[1] etc., some anonymous dweller in darkness, a fervent but wretched defender of Remonstranto-Socinianism (as is apparent from the writing), after attacking, not without a panoply of insults and slanders, sometimes me and my disputation, and sometimes especially our religion and church, then calmly rejected, among several other assertions of mine, also this one about organ music, without any examination, as if it were groundless. When I answered him on the heels of that,[2] I responded in a little book entitled *Thersites*[3] *Heautontimorumenos, seu Remonstrantium hyperaspistes etc. Retusus etc.*, in part 3, chapter 3, page 293: *I wiped away*

---

1. Batelier, *Examen accuratum*.
2. κατά πόδας.
3. See *Iliad of Homer*, Book II, lines 212–24. Voetius implies that his opponent is a rabble rouser, even as he demonstrates his own intellectual refinement and moral nobility in contrast to his opponent who is an ignoble person of mythic proportions!

that aspersion of groundlessness in this way [by saying], *It is not groundless to air a controversy between us and the papists, and one indeed of such a kind which pertains to religious practice and worship. Concerning this [controversy], see Bellarmine, book 1* Concerning Good Works, *especially chapter 17, and Thomas* [Summa Theologiae] *22, question 91, article 2, and on the same matter, Cajetan as well in his* Summula, *page 519. And from our people, see Beza on the Colloquy of Montbéliard*[4] *part 2, William Zepper,* Politica Ecclesiastica[5] *book 4, chapter 9, as well as Master [André] Rivet in his* Prolegomena on a Decad of the Psalms,[6] *where he says, when about to deal with this question:* There has been doubt about organ music in times past, and even at this time there is controversy about whether it should be employed and brought back in the Church. *Tilenus in the*

4. = Théodore de Bèza (1519-1605), *Acta colloquii Montis Belligartensis.*

5. = Wilhelm Zepper (1550-1607), *Politia Ecclesiastica,* I:XV:175: [Margin: *De Musica instrumentali, & organis.*] *Minimè omnium autem tolerabitur in ecclesiâ Musica instrumentalis, & organa illa Musica confragosa, quæ varium vocum garritum efficiunt, & templa lituis, tubis, & fistulis personare faciunt. Quorum Vitalianum Pontificem, primum auctorem fuisse Platina affirmat. Fuit hoc circa annum Christi. 690, vel secundúm alios 770. Judæi quidem omnis generis instrumentis Musicus penes cultum suum usi fuerunt. Verúm Chrystostomus in Psal. 150 hac dereita scribit: Judæis, inquit, ideó diversos sonos fuerat at habere permissum, propter infirmatatem cordis sui, ut organis saltem immutati, ad charitatem invitarentur. Et divinâ permibione fuit, ut qui deliciosis mentibus tepida cogitabant, & dibimulationis negligentiâ prememebantur, voluptuariis conversationibus inhærentes, sic saltem aliquid spernerent vanitatis. Pauló anté veró inquit: Sicut Judæi jubebantur omnis organi sono laudere Dominum: sic no omni corpore laudare properemus, oculus, linguæ, auribus, manibus hoc debemus essicere. Et sic homo cithará, corde, membro, & sonos canticorum conscentiæ imitetur affectu, & animus magister attendat, & pulset pectora, & sonus reddetur ad coelum.*

6. = André Rivet (1572-1651), *Commentarius in Psalmorum.* Though Voetius refers to Rivet's ten (*decad*) Psalm discussions, the work actually covers twelve (*dodecadem*).

Syntagma, *disputation 49*,[7] *and the* Altar of Damascus,[8] *Chapter 8 page 491. Just so, the question of organs is proposed to our reformers by Cudsemius (if I am not mistaken) in* On the Desperate Cause of Calvin[9] *and by Eckhard in his* Little Collection of Controversies *chapter 21, question 5. Now you see the usefulness of our question. Furthermore, the daily noise of organs in our churches warns us to instill these precautions diligently into the common people, so that they may not think that the organist is an ecclesiastical minister, or that the sound of organs is religious worship—as indeed some of the more ignorant sort might easily believe, along with the papacy....*

Voetius ends the *Appendix* much the same way he began:

Now let the reader judge whether my assertion was groundless, as well as the various precautions of the first theologians, of the medieval ones, and of the latest ones of our Reformation. Provoked nearly twenty-eight years ago by my Remonstrant attacker, a dweller in darkness, I answered that these things had to be repeated to and instilled into the common people. I have made a declaration about these things to this extent: that it is not of such great importance to us, as if in them the highest principle of

---

7. = Daniel Tilenus (1563–1633), *Syntagmatis tripertiti disputationum*, 793: 49. *Instrumenta inanimata, siue ea sint* ψηλάφητα, *siue* ἁ ἐμπνευζα, *quicunque in Ecclesiam revocant, Synagogam pridem sepultam, hac in parte refodiunt nam ad Leviticum cultum ista pertinuisse nos afferimus, freti loco 2. Chro. 29. 25. neque verò Davidis exemplo niti possunt qui Nathanis, id est, Prophetæ præcepto, illud imitati non iubentur. Et institutum hoc alienum ab Ecclesia esse, non modò veteres adfirmant, qui eiusmodi crepitacula pueros magis decere aiunt, quàm viros, quos par est* τά το νηπία καταργείν. *Iustin quast. 107. Verum etiam Scholastici, qui apertè hoc vocant Iudaizare.* Thom.2.2.q.91.art.2. Caiet. ibid. | 50. *Operosum illud miachinaementu, quod antonomasticè vocant Organon, Vitaliani Papę inventum, ac donum, illis arrideat, qui magnę Meretrici supparasitari, quàm Christianę simplicitari studere malunt: non absimiles Ethnicis, quos Lactantius ad templa ventitare ait, non tam religionis gratia, quam ut videant & audient, quod oblecter lib.2.c.7. & quibus publicorum conuentuum finis non est* παιδεία, *sed* παιδιά.

8. = David Calderwood (1575–1650), *The altar of Damascus or the patern of the English hierarchie, and Church policie obtruded upon the Church of Scotland* (Amsterdam: Giles Thorpe, 1621). The title *Altar of Damascus* is a reference to 2 Kings 16:10–18. There, King Ahaz of Judah saw an altar in Damascus when he went to visit Tiglath-pileser; he liked it so well that he asked the priest Uriah to build a copy at Jerusalem, and to offer the principal offerings for the king and the people on it. He then had Solomon's original altar moved to a different place in the temple.

9. Petrus Cudsemius (?–1649), *Tractatus Brevis, De Desperata Calvini Causa: Lectu non minus utilis, atque iucundus; In Quo Sectae Calvinisticae non tam picta effigies, quam vivum corpus, cuivis spectandum ad oculum exhibetur* (Coloniae: Gualterus, 1612).

the faith[10] or of some fundamental article would be overturned, and as if no tolerance, unity fellowship, or fraternity could exist between churches which disagreed here in practice or even in opinion. I was only obliged to and desired to defend the better and safer way,[11] which the Reformed theologians already cited are showing, from the attack of the adversaries already cited, and [to defend] my harmless assertion, proposed in the year 1635 and defended against *Thersites*, once more against an accusation of contradiction and absurdity.

10. *summa fidei*.
11. *tutiorem*.

MARTIN SCHOOK

Organ Music in Churches (1663)

Alas, there is no evidence that this theological advice effected any change of practice in Voetius's Utrecht. To the contrary, much evidence suggests that Utrecht churches continued to use their pipe organs (if the church still had one) and that organ use possibly even increased. Among the loudest voices leading Reformed churches away from Voetius's position and toward including pipe organ music in worship was his student Martin Schoock. Born a generation after Voetius, Schoock was first a student of Voetius in Utrecht, then a professor in Deventer, Groningen, and finally at Frankfurt upon Oder, where he died in 1665 at the age of fifty-one.[1] In 1663, Schoock published a telling—and daring—orgelist article that challenged his mentor. Claiming that Voetius is "pseudo-faithful" to his sources, Schoock builds his own case for pipe organ inclusion in services of Reformed worship.

***Exercitationes variae, de viersis* [de diversis] *materiis, quae hac edition* [editione] *nova tum locupletate* [locupletatae] *et vindicatae* [sunt]. Trajecti ad Rhenum: Gisbertus à Zyll, 1663. *De Musica Organica in templis*, 515–39:**

I. The occasion of this controversy in the Netherlands is noted. Before the issue in dispute is formulated, it is shown how misleadingly Master Voetius, who has another opinion on this point, has cited certain authors. No one is

---

1. Van der Aa et al., *Biographisch woordenboek*, 396–98.

such a foreigner in the Netherlands that he does not know that the orthodox churches in that fortunate region have begun to be disturbed, since the forty-first year of this century, by those men who, opinionated as they are,[2] do not permit, in matters which are in themselves indifferent, any other usage than the one which corresponds exactly to their own preconceived opinion. They also want to avoid appearing to plead their case for this opinion. In that year a truly noble man, Master Constantinus Huygens, governor of Zulich, who was also at that time in the privy council of the most illustrious Prince of Orange Henricus Fredericus, had brought out in the Dutch language a little book, *On the use and abuse of organs*.[3] Although he pointed out various misuses of the pipe organ as it is played in various churches in the Netherlands, he contended with erudition (if it be granted that this can be preserved) that psalm-singing must be guided, as it often is disorderly because of the inexperience of the people. As this little book was sent by its eminent author to various people, among the Dutch theologians Master Johannes Polyander, a principal theologian in the school at Leyden, Ludovicus de Dieu, and Abrahamus Heidanus, very great and celebrated men, and at that same time ministers of the divine Word, approved it completely;[4] and among other professors, men famous throughout the whole world, Daniel Heinsius, Adolphus Vorstius, and Jacobus Golius, besides very many other men who were very renowned both in politics and in the Church. Their responses were published together in the same year. Master Gisbertus Voetius, the Utrecht theologian, had also been consulted, but he held his judgment in abeyance for the time being, content to write back on the eighth day before the Ides of March[5] 1641: *Indeed I would have liked to write my opinion out now in full, if certain other works in preparation, whose publication now is pressing, did not hinder me. And I would reserve this entire matter, whatever it is, for a more precise discussion to be published some other time.* In the same year this reverend gentleman also presented what he had promised, by presenting two disputations, held on July 3 and 10, *On organs and organ music in worship*, the respondent being Johannes Heimenbergius, at that time a reverend pastor in the same place. The theme of the debate, Th[esis] 3, was in this form: *The question is whether instrumental music or organ music, whether by itself or combined with vocal*

---

2. ἰδιογνώμονες.
3. = Constantijn Huygens (1596–1687), *Gebruyck of ongebruyck*.
4. ὁ πάνο.
5. 7 March.

music, is either a necessary or at least a useful part of public worship in the Church; or whether it is either a part or an act of religion; at least a mode, need, means [or] support for public worship, or practiced communally in the New Testament Church, and therefore in conformity with Divine authority. As he himself answers in the negative, so he cites, according to his custom and his faithfulness (that is, with Voetian pseudo-faithfulness), various orthodox theologians as if they are of the same opinion[6] as himself, to support his opinion. But before we define the exact status of the dispute, it would be useful to have cited some of these theologians, whereby it would then become apparent both with what "faithfulness" the reverend gentleman cited them, and how the status of the controversy can be suitably framed according to those theologians. I would start with Calvin, if the noble Master Huygens himself had not shown on page 73 and following of his little book that he [Calvin] was not opposed to organs completely, but only as far as a hypothesis that they do nothing for edification. From this, I come next to Musculus;[7] as he is praised by the reverend gentleman for the commentary on chapter 14 of the first letter of Paul to the Corinthians, so I only come upon the following, on verse 7: *It is not established in what use the tibia and cithara were among the Corinthians in Paul's time, I think; nevertheless it is clear enough, because the apostle proves something by them in this place, that they were known and frequently used by the common people,* etc. (these things can be safely omitted because they concern the various uses of musical instruments among different nations). *However, it is not the case that in this place of the apostle we may defend the pleasures of musical organs, stealthily introduced in Papist churches, which he certainly would never have approved, nor indeed would the pagans who were zealous for a severer discipline.*[8] Then [Lambertus] Danaeus, who was cited from part 4, chapter 26 of his *Isagoge[s Christianae]*, has nothing of which he [Voetius] can approve except what is contained in the following words: *Certainly it now appears that from the very times of the apostles, the custom and usage of singing in church was publicly accepted; not such, to be sure, as there is today in Catholic*

---

6. ὁμόψηφοι.

7. = Wolfgang Musculus (1497–1563), *In ambas Apostoli Pauli*, 544: *Quo in usu tempore Pauli suerint apud Corinthios tibia & cithara, non constat, ut opinor: notas tamen & usitatas vulgo fuisse, satis ex illo patet, quod ab illis argumentatur hoc loco Apostollus.*

8. Musculus, *In ambas Apostoli Pauli*, 544: *Non est autem ut hoc Apostoli loco defendamus delicias organorum musicorum, templis Papistarum subintroductas, quas san nunquam probavissent, ne Ethnici quidem, severioris disciplinae studiosi.*

churches.⁹ In the theses which he proposed to the Lutherans at the Colloquy of Montbéliard, held in the year 1586, [Théodore de] Bèze has this: *We do not at all condemn music because music pertains to organs, but where there is singing in harmony; for the mind does not comprehend it, and the thing itself shows what follows: little by little, a great part of the worship of God is transformed into ditties, and minds are not fed by the word of God, but ears are soothed by empty sounds.* And further, in his annotations on the marginal notes of Jacobus Andreas: *God forbid that we should reprove the legitimate use of music, either when prepared for honest delight, or especially for singing the praises of God. But Christians do not have holy assemblies for the sake of such pleasure, nor will Master Andreas ever have persuaded us to follow his counsels. Rather, we should listen to the apostle: if he rightly forbade in the church assembly the custom of speaking in strange tongues without an interpreter, he would have tolerated much less in the church those harmonic sounds of music, by which the ears alone are stimulated, since they are not understood in any way as they are being sung, even by those who sing them often.* Likewise Perkinsus,¹⁰ presented in the *Problema Theologica* page 365, has only this: *Pipe instruments had their beginning around the year of our Lord 660 (Platina in* Vitaliano*) or 820 (Aimonus,* De Gestis Francorum *book 4, chapter 114). In* Liber de oratione et horis canonicis, *chapter 16, Navarre, says that the use of organs had not yet been accepted in the time of Aquinas. Modulation of the singing*¹¹ *was condemned by Gregory in book 4, letter 44 of* De gestis Synodi habitae in Urbe.¹² The words of Piscator¹³ in the

---

9. *Apparet certe jam inde ab ipsis Apostolorum temporibus morem consuetudinemque cantandi in Ecclesia fuisse publice receptum, non quails quidem hodie est in Ecclesiis Papisticis.*

10. = William Perkins (1558–1602), *Guil. Perkinsi Problema*, 364ff: *Instrumenta Pneumatica ortum habuerunt circa ann. Cathedral. DCLX. Platina in Vitaliano. vel anno DCCCXX. Aimonius de gestis Franc. lib. 4. c. 114. Navarrus in lib. de Oration. & Horis Canon. cap. 16 ait, temporibus Aquinatis usum Organorum nondum receptum fuisse. Cantus modulatio im probata est à Gregorio lib. 4. epist. 44. de gestis Synodi habitae in urbe.*

11. *cantus modulatio.*

12. *Opera D. Gregorii Papae*, II:1459.

13. = Johannes Piscator (Johann Fischer 1546–1625), *In librum Psalmorum*, 199–200: *In congregatione ecclesiastica decet Deum laudare cantu. Sed quaeritur, an in novo testamento ad cantum ecclesiasticum adhibenda etiam sint instrumenta musica, ut adhibebantur tempore Davidis, & deinceps in veteri testament? Ratio dubitandi est, quòd ille canendi modus videtur fuisse pars pædagogia Mosaicae. Respondeo: Quum talis canendi modus nui quam à Deo praeceptus sit, nec veritus: apparet natur☒ su☒ ἀδιάφορον esse. Sed interim videtur, novo testament magis convenire cantus simplex vocalis: quippe ad quem solum Paulus hortatur fideles Ephesios, Ephes.5.v.19. Item fideles Colossenses, Coloβ.3.v.16.*

observations on Psalm 33 are as follows: *It is fitting to praise God with song in the church's assembly. But there is a question: Should musical instruments also be added to the song of the church in the New Testament, as they were added in the time of David and regularly in the Old Testament? There is reason to doubt that this method of singing seemed to have been part of Mosaic teaching. I answer: Since this method of singing was neither commanded nor forbidden by God, it appears to be indifferent in nature. But in the meantime, it appears that simple vocal melody was more suitable to the New Testament. Indeed, Paul exhorts the Ephesian believers to this alone (Ephesians 5:19), and likewise the Colossian believers (Colossians 3:16). For even if in his words to the Ephesians he uses the word* psallein, *which means to sing with stringed instruments, nevertheless he also seems to mean singing, where the holy psalms are sung with the mouth.* Thus far says Piscator. Rivet in his *Prolegomena to the Psalms* comments: *We consider the use of organs as a matter of adiaphora, although I would rather recommend it be removed completely from the churches, lest some come to church not so much for the sake of religion as for the purpose of seeing and hearing what is pleasant. Under this name Lactantius reproves the pagans in the* Divine Institutes, *book 2, chapter 7; and Erasmus, the great ornament of Holland, in the* Annotations *to chapter 14 of 1 Corinthians, complains that "a type of labored and theatrical music had been introduced in holy places of worship, such as he does not think had ever been heard in the theaters of the Greeks and Romans: everything reverberated with trumpets, horns, flutes, and harps." What is done in certain Netherlands Reformed churches can be tolerated, where the organs lead the communal singing of the people, lest discord result from the ignorance of many. Nevertheless, we should be wary, lest under such a pretext the misuse might return again.* Rivet also says this. No one will be surprised that Pareus[14] and Coppenius,[15] the Palatine theologians, equally cited by Master Voetius, were hostile to organ music, if he observes that they were members of a church which outlawed organs from churches as a whole. The same thing would be thought about Master Altingius, formerly their colleague and now among the saints,[16] who in his *Exegesis on the Augsburg Confession*[17]

Nam etsi in dicto ad Ephes. utitur verbo ψάλλειν, *quod significat canere sidibus: tamen videtur eo significare cantum, quo Psalmi sacri canuntur ore.*

14. = David Pareus (1548–1622).
15. = Bartholomaeus Coppen (1565–1617).
16. τῷ ἐν ἁγίοις.
17. = Heinrich Alting (1583–1644), *Exegesis logica*.

has followed closely their footsteps, seeing that they were his own colleagues at the University of Heidelberg. However, I have never heard that this reverend man, who for many years was an elder of the church at Groningen, was a follower of this practice; for since the time when the orthodox faith was publicly accepted, he was always in charge of the organ and kept the church singing in order. And so, because of different times and places, wise men tend to favor different opinions about those things which in themselves are *adiaphora*. The same would be thought about Zepper, who is called to give his opinion ahead of others in this controversy by the author of the *Altar of Damascus*, the *hyperaspis*[18] of Master Voetius. I have less to say about Tilenus, for when he wrote those things which laugh at Master Voetius no less than at the author of the *Altar of Damascus*, he will have composed those same things for the occasion of his installation at the University of Sedan. But I am not the one to doubt that he began to be a very great supporter of organs, of which he had disapproved earlier, from the time when he undertook to write the provocative recommendation for the hierarchy in the kingdom of England. But it is especially strange that Master Voetius undertook to ascribe something to this "companion of Ecebolius"[19] when he himself, while only the minister of the church at Heusden, had censured in a satiric manner, to the point of reproach to the author, that same person's virulent writing against the five articles of the Synod of Dordt. However, from these very theologians praised by Master Voetius, we may draw these four conclusions: 1. That the use of organs in a holy congregation is *adiaphoros*. 2. That they are not allowed to be used to delight the ears to the extent that this is usually done in Papist churches. 3. That the use of these organs was not instituted by Christ himself or by his apostles; nor was it even accepted in the early Church. 4. That organs can be legitimately allowed to guide the singing of the church assembly; otherwise there would be discord. So the primary question is this: whether pipe organs in the Reformed churches, when solemnly and suitably regulated, can serve to guide the singing of the church congregation, which otherwise usually produces dissonant melodies? As I answer this question in the affirmative, so, with God's good help, I will construct our response so solidly (after saying some things first), that I shall simultaneously answer all the arguments of Master Voetius just as solidly.

---

18. One who holds a protecting shield over another.
19. Someone who has changed his opinion.

1 | PROFESSORS

II. Instrumental music in the Old Testament was instituted and set in order by David, according to the command of his prophets. Now I do not wish to discuss here the praises of music, both vocal and instrumental. This has been done quite often by others, and is less suitable for my purpose. Before everything else, it is appropriate to consider for what reason instrumental music was accepted in the worship of the Old Testament itself. And just as God, through Moses, ordained ceremonial worship, so he gave silver trumpets to the priests (Numbers 10:1–2), by which the people were called together to the assembly, and the leaders to be consulted about the nation. Likewise they gave the signal for moving the camp. For calling the people, they sounded both; for the leaders, one; but if the camp had to be moved, they sounded with a loud clamor. In addition, for use in the year of Jubilee, Joel was sounding the *shofar*; whether this was a trumpet or a ram's horn, or if the sound of whatever horn was longer drawn out, or even if the ringing call of the trumpet was longer drawn out, is of no consequence to us, but see Bernardus Fullenius,[20] most learned in Middle Eastern languages, in book 4 chapter 8 of the *Miscellanea*. This is certain, that there was no use of musical instruments in the rites of the Israelite people outside of the ordinance of God through Moses, who fully ordained ceremonial worship. King David first instituted this near the end of his reign (or in its fortieth year, as Usserius[21] well observes in the *Chronologia Sacra*). Although David was the *sweet psalm-singer among the Israelites* (2 Samuel 23:1), he appointed certain people *to the service of music in the house of the Lord* (1 Chronicles 6:31), who *prophesied* (that is, performed everything among the musicians according to the prescription of David, who had written down the psalms earlier, as a prophet, for them; for so this saying is also received in Ezra 3:10–11, 2 Chronicles 29:25) *with* cymbala, nablia, *and* citharae" (1 Chronicles 25:1), and thus far *They applied themselves to music in the house of the Lord with* cymbala, nablia, *and* citharae, *for the service of God* (verse 6). Wherefore Nehemiah 12:24 also says that indeed this ordinance is to be ascribed to David alone, concerning the Levite singers: *they should praise and celebrate, following the precept of David, the man of God*. At the same time I hear from the theologian Rainoldus,[22] very great in a former era, in his Lecture 187 on the apocryphal books, that David did this because of a specific *precept of the Lord and his prophets*. For although it is certain that David was king

---

20. = Bernardus Fullenius (1602–1657).
21. = James Ussher (1581–1656), *Annales Veteris Testamenti*.
22. = John Rainolds (1549–1607), *Censura Librorvm Apocryphorum*, 2:907ff.

and that it pertained to his office *that everything should be done decently and in order in the house of the Lord*²³ (1 Corinthians 14:40), he himself also speaks of himself thus (Psalm 119:99–100): *I have become wiser than all my teachers, because your testimonies are my meditation; I am more knowing than the elders, because I keep your commandments.* So by virtue of his holy experience he could distribute the duties of singing among the Levites, because he judged that this would be of service no less to their order than to the glory of God. But he did this by the special revelation which was made to his own prophets, that it might appear brighter than noonday, according to 2 Chronicles 29:25, where the Scripture speaks of Hezekiah: *He had reinstated the Levites in the house of the Lord, with* cymbala, *with* nablia, *and with* citharae, *according to the precept of David, and of Gad the king's seer, and of Nathan the prophet: for this precept was from God, through his prophets.* Nevertheless it will become clear later that it will not be prejudicial to us that this instrumental music, and the very order which the royal prophet established among the Levites, has a rationale of no greater type. Later, in its own place, there will be a discussion whether this music truly was of service to the untrained state of the people of Israel.

III. How was singing in public accepted in the New Testament churches? Coming to the New Testament, in it singing is not enjoined to the faithful except as a private exercise. This is clear in all places where singing is mentioned. In 1 Corinthians 14:15 the apostle, speaking of himself, says: *I will sing with the spirit, and I will sing with the understanding also.* And in Ephesians 5:18–19 he speaks to the Ephesian faithful thus: *Do not be intoxicated with wine, in which is debauchery, but be filled with the Spirit, speaking to one another.*²⁴ Likewise he says to the Colossians in chapter 3 verse 16: *Let the word of Christ dwell within you richly with all wisdom, teaching and admonishing one another*²⁵ *with psalms and hymns and spiritual songs, with thanksgiving, singing to the Lord in your heart.* Also the apostle James says in chapter 5 verse 13: *Let anyone with a glad heart sing.* All these concern the private exercises of Christians, but by no means those which were to be enacted in the church assembly. Peter Martyr [Vermigli] rightly saw this the same way in his commentary on chapter 14 of 1 Corinthians, for in a dispute about church singing, after

---

23. Schoock's italics here include the phrase *in the house of the Lord*, but that phrase is not in 1 Corinthians 14:40.

24. ἑαυτοῖς.

25. ἑαυτούς.

he had cited the preceding words of Paul from the letter to the Ephesians, he added this: *where you may see that Christians are advised to sing for themselves and in their own hearts. Therefore, as far as sacred assemblies are concerned, nothing is gained from this.* Nor do I listen to Beza, who explains Ephesians 5's ἑαυτοῖς as ἀλλήλοις, that the sense is *mutually among yourselves*, and that singing in gatherings is involved; and somehow he is mistaken about the place in Colossians. Thus far plain singing in church had not truly been prescribed by the apostle, but it has come into use by custom, as was also known to Augustine; about this you may read in his work, in book 10 chapter 33 of the *Confessions*: *I am drawn to approve the custom of singing in the church.* Originally it was accepted in the Eastern churches, then by the Western churches, according to the antiphons which Ambrose first made use of at Milan. This same Augustine is a witness in book 9 chapter 7 of the *Confessions*, where as he records what he saw in Milan, among other things he has this, as follows: *Then the singing of hymns and psalms according to the manner of the Eastern regions was instituted, lest the people be consumed by the weariness of their mourning; and this has been retained from that time to the present day, with many flocks of yours, and really almost all of them throughout the rest of the world, copying it.* However, the custom grew strong in the Eastern churches not long after the time of the apostles. Pliny the Younger, proconsul of Bithynia and Pontus, was a witness of this in that famous letter to Trajan, which is no. 97 in book 10.[26] Tertullian, looking back at it in his *Apology*, chapter 2, says: *Plinius Secundus, when he was ruling over the province, after condemning some Christians and driving some away from their position, was nevertheless so troubled by their multitude that he then consulted the emperor Trajan about what he should do about the rest, stating that aside from their obstinacy in not sacrificing, he had learned nothing else about their sacred rites except about the meetings before dawn to sing to Christ and God, and to gather for teaching, which forbade murder, adultery, theft, deceit, and other crimes.* See! He makes mention of singing, which was used frequently in the predawn meetings. Jerome refers to the same thing in the *Chronicles of Eusebius*, when he writes under the year 123, the tenth year of Trajan's reign: *Plinius Secundus asked Trajan what he should do, telling him that*

---

26. = Pliny Secundus (62–115), *Epistularum libri decem*, 642: *adfirmabant autem hanc fuisse summam vel culpae suae vel erroris, quod essent soliti stato die ante lucem convenire carmenque Christo quasi deo dicere secum invicem seque sacramento non in scelus aliquod obstringere, sed ne furta, ne latrocinia, ne adulteria committerent, ne fidem fallerent, ne depositum appellati abnegarent.*

aside from their obstinacy in not sacrificing, and the predawn meetings to sing to a certain Christ as to a god, he found out nothing else about them. So they really did sing, to encourage one another by singing. Therefore Tertullian adds in chapter 39 of the *Apology*, after he had talked about the love-feasts:[27] *After the washing of hands, lights are also lit, so that each one may be called forward in the midst to sing to God from the Holy Scriptures or from his own understanding.* And he writes similarly in the second book of *Ad Uxorem*: *As they repeatedly did, not only at the love-feasts, but also at ordinary meals.* Cyprian is a witness in book 2, letter 2 (this is the letter to Donatus, from which, cultivated and combed as it is, Augustine in book 4, chapter 14 of *De doctrina Christiana* seeks an example of splendid and felicitous diction), when he says as follows: *Let the temperate meal resound with psalms; as your memory is retentive and your voice melodious, undertake this service, as your custom is. You will nourish your dearest friends more, if when we hear something spiritual, sacred sweetness allures our ears.* Later on, psalmists[28] were accepted; what their office was, Isidore refers to when he says in book 2, chapter 13 of *On Ecclesiastical Offices: to the psalmist belongs the office of singing, saying the blessings, the psalms, the praises, the responses of the sacrifice, and whatever pertains to the knowledge of singing*, and, in the chapter above, he traces them back to those ancient psalmists who *sang alone continually in the temple, wearing white robes, while the choir responded to their voices.* There were very many of them, especially in the church at Constantinople, whose leader is called πρωτοψάλτης by Justinian in *Novellae Constitutiones* 3, and by the Latins, *primicerius cantorum*,[29] as has been already noted by many.

IV. The question is, when instrumental music was accepted in the New Testament churches, [and] what is *psallein*? Among learned men it is disputed whether, besides plain singing, instrumental [music] was also accepted in the early Church out of custom (just as the other also was). That it was banished from places of worship, they openly strive to prove from Justin Martyr, who by the interpretation of Perionius[30] in question 107 proposed by the gentiles argues thus: *Singing isn't fit only for children; but singing with lifeless instruments, and with dancing and castanets, is. Therefore the use of instruments of this type, and of others which are fit for children, has been*

27. *agapis*.
28. *psalmistæ*.
29. Head of the singers.
30. = Joachim Périon (1499–1559).

driven out of places of worship and done away with. Suppose that I don't say now along with Possevinus[31] that this work of *146 Questions* does not look like it should be attributed to Justin as author; further, that Justin is not utterly condemning organ music in churches, but music which is trifling, wanton, and superstitious; therefore he says *with dancing and castanets.*[32] For Prudentius, the Christian poet, is an extremely credible witness that the ancient Christians celebrated the praises of God with musical instruments also, in his *Apotheosis*, v. 454ff.:[33]

> *Whatever the curved trumpet resounds, echoing in the hollow air;*
> *whatever the mighty breath pours out from hidden inhalation;*
> *whatever the chaste lyre, whatever the cithern rings out;*
> *what the harmonious pipes [organa] of uneven reeds intermingle;*
> *what the rival caverns of shepherds give back with voices;*
> *it celebrates Christ, it resounds Christ; all things,*
> *even mute ones, are speaking, given life by holy strings.*

Yes indeed, I consider it most persuasive that the apostle Paul himself taught this to the Ephesians in the place mentioned since indeed he not only says ᾄδοντες but adds ψάλλοντες, which really cannot be considered synonymous. So also in Colossians 3 he distinctly thinks of ψαλμῶν, ὕμνων, καὶ ᾠδῶν. From the ancient writers, Jerome on Ephesians 5 and Chrysostom on Colossians 3 are consulted about the difference among these; from the more recent, Beza, toward the end. Now although, in place of this in Ephesians 5, Ephrem the Syrian[34] had ᾄδειν καὶ ψάλλειν, for all that they differ, the apostle also wanted to signify something with ψάλλειν, because it is not ἐν τῷ ᾄδεω. Not only his *Etymology* but also the *Glossary*, explaining that, will teach what ψάλλειν means. About that, the author of the *Etymologicus Magnus*[35] says this: ψάλλειν, ἐπὶ τῶν χορδῶν τῆς λύρας

---

31. = Antonio Possevino (1533–1611).
32. μετὰ ὀρχήσεως καὶ κροτάλων.
33. = Aurelius Prudentius Clemens (348–405), *Liber Apotheosis*, 35:
quidquid in aere cavo reboans tuba curva remugit,
quidquid ab arcano vomit ingens spiritus haustu,
quidquid casta chelys, quidquid testudo resultat,
organa disparibus calamis quod consona miscent,
aemula pastorum quod reddunt vocibus antra,
Christum concelebrat, Christum sonat, omnia Christum
muta etiam fidibus sanctis animata loquuntur.
34. = Ephrem Syrus (306–373).
35. *Etymologicon magnum.*

παρὰ τὸ προσεγγίζω, ὁυ προσάγωγον ψάυω. There he expressly signifies that ψάλλειν is the same thing as gently touching, by playing, the strings of the lyre or of another musical instrument. Indeed, in the *Glossary* these words appear: φάλλω, *nabizo, psalmizo;* φαλτήριον, *sambucum;* ψάλτης: *nablio, psalta.* These abundantly serve to confirm my opinion.

V. It does not seem that the organ was accepted in the Western churches before AD 766. Nevertheless, instrumental music for so-called "public" use was not accepted in the Christian church in the first centuries. The Papists themselves, otherwise very attached to the claim of antiquity, acknowledge this. Let me not cite others; one, Bellarmine, will have been the model for very many others. In book 1 of *De bonis operibus*, shortly before the end of chapter 17, he sets out his opinion about organs as ecclesiastical: *We acknowledge that the use of musical instruments has not been so fitting for perfect and imperfect people, and so it began to be permitted later in the Church; for the use of organs in the church began first in the time of Pope Vitalian, circa. AD 660, if we believe Platina; but if we wish to trust Aimonius in book 4, chapter 114 of* De gestis Francorum, *organs were not heard in churches before the time of Louis the Pious, that is after AD 1320.* Thus Bellarmine. Baronius, a contemporary[36] of Bellarmine, and extremely versed in ecclesiastical antiquities, attests that the organ was brought from the East to the West in the year AD 766, by the legates of Constantinus [V] Copronymus, when Pepin was involved with the synod in Gaul. We accept these things, and as accepted, they are taken to serve our purpose. In turn, it is appropriate to point out with separate assertions that the Papists themselves are accustomed to argue about the same things with respect to singing, no less plain singing than singing with organs, just as it is frequently done in church congregations.

VI. The Papists also desire many things in common with us, concerning vocal music. Therefore, when Bochellus, in book 1 of the *Decisions of the French Church*, quotes the Council of Bourges, held in France in the year 1584, it had made this statement: *As the Church was growing, the use of singing and playing instruments in public was accepted and observed, first in the Eastern churches, and at length in the Western, for the purpose of stirring and arousing the affection of souls which were growing listless and sluggish.* And the Council of Sens, already in the year 1528, decreed thus: *Popular and lascivious melodies are not to be heard in the churches under the pretext of being musical song.* And again, at the Council of Bordeaux

36. σύνχρονος.

in the year 1582: *Let any music having to do with anything lascivious, and vulgar melodies, or frivolity and similar follies, be completely kept away from the organs and church singing; but let it be serious everywhere, and fit for the praises of God, so that the souls of the faithful bystanders are kindled by it to greater piety, devotion, and religion.* In these synodical decrees the Papist doctors themselves stipulate this, at least those in whom there still survives a little bit of honest shame. In *Catholicus Orthodoxus*, volume 2, question 36, Master Rivet has cited, besides Cajetan, Lindanus, bishop of Roermond, who in book 4 of his *Panoplia evangelica* gravely addresses and seriously laments these issues, saying this, among other things: *Wherefore* (he says) *I admire the constancy of those churches who, foreseeing this abuse of divine worship, have preferred to prohibit this music to the choir, as at Utrecht and at Lyons (as I hear), more than I honor that magnificent majesty of those* (he is indicating other churches) *which they think and boast of so much. With this they seem to themselves, very plainly, to have filled God's choir with every arrangement of choristers, with the division of every type of voices, nay, also with the clangor of trumpets, the blare of horns, and other various noise, lest they seem to omit something that at one and the same time obscures the words of the song and buries and overwhelms its meaning.* Bellarmine himself agrees, for, while writing on Psalm 46, he appends these words, among others: *The word* sapienter *means, as Augustine and Chrysostom advise, that whoever sings the psalms should understand what he is singing; and from the understanding of hidden things, the affection of devotion may be moved toward God. At the present time, those who have undertaken the office of singing in the Church have not sinned lightly in this matter.* And even more clearly he displays his thoughts about the title of the same psalm, when he says: *The title counsels the sons of Korah, to whom it was given to sing the psalms, to understand what they sing, and to cause their hearers to understand. This counsel is to be committed to memory for church singers. For singing in the Church ought to be of service to the spirit, and not just to the delight of the ears. For just as those who sing intelligently and devoutly ravish the souls of the hearers, so those who bring theatrical tunes into the Church make a worldly stage out of the house of God.* Indeed, this counsel concerns vocal music no less than instrumental. By reason of this, if the Papists themselves find fault with everything that smells of the stage, then this same thing should likewise be much more displeasing to the Reformed. For already in his own century Jerome rightly wrote, while commenting on Ephesians chapter 5: *Let the young people listen, let those* listen whose office it is to make music in the Church, lest after the manner of tragedians they anoint their throats and gullets with sweet embellishment, and lest theatrical melodies be heard in the Church.

VII. It is explained in greater detail what things concerning ecclesiastical singing should be attended to. Now with reference to vocal music itself, even more and other things must be guarded against; which[Justin] Martyr especially touches upon, when he writes about 1 Corinthians 14 as follows: *In ancient times, this was the lowest gift in the Church, committed to the people, the* psalmista, *and the* lector; *but now it seems to be taking the leading roles. A second fault also must be guarded against: lest it* (that is, the singing) *take over the greater and better parts of the liturgy. Where it is too highly regarded, this happens, so that somehow there is no place left for doctrine and instruction. For today we often see it happen on great feasts, that because of the many ceremonies and the abundant music, the gathering is prolonged until noon, when human beings are sleepy and less attentive. In addition, it must be seen to that the singing is not so broken up and uneven that it will hinder the perception of the senses. Nor should this fault be committed: that singers are given such large stipends that the wealth which belongs to the more useful ministers and to the poor may be used up.* Thus far Martyr. But just as these things should be guarded against, so other observations should be made concerning singing (I do not wish to speak just now of the object of this), as legitimately instituted, from the advice of Scripture itself. 1. The particular instrument of song should be the heart, as is clear from Ephesians 5 and Colossians 3, already cited above. It is not as if the tongue should be mute, but because preparation of the heart should precede the tongue's breaking forth into some divine song. Therefore the royal Psalmist, as often as he makes himself ready to sing, not only prepares his voice or his harp, but his heart, ahead of and before them. Wherefore Psalm 57:8–9 says: *My heart is ready, O God, my heart is ready; I will sing and utter a psalm to the Lord; awake, psaltery and cithara,* etc. And Psalm 71:22–23: *I will celebrate you with the harp, I will play for you on the cithara, O Holy One of Israel, my lips will sing when I play for you, and my soul, which you will redeem.* Thus the blessed virgin sang in her heart, at the same time when she broke into these words: *My soul magnifies the Lord, and my spirit rejoices in God my Savior.* Accordingly, Bernard in sermon 52, *De modo bene vivendi,* says: *When in the sight of God you are singing psalms and hymns, keep in your mind what you are singing with your voice; do not think about one thing and sing another. If you sing one thing in your mind and another with your voice, you are losing the fruit of your labor. If your body is standing in the church, and your mind is wandering around outside, you are losing your reward.* Wherefore it is said: "This people honors me with their lips, but their heart is far from me."[37] For thus says the Apostle: *"I will make music with the spirit, and will make music with the mind also. I will sing with the heart and with my mouth."*[38] For it is good to glorify God with the sound of the voice, and with hymns, and psalms, and spiritual songs. Just as we are helped by prayers, so we are delighted by the melodies of the psalms. 2. However, in order for someone to be able to sing with the heart, before everything else, the heart has to be purified. As for those who presume to sing to the Lord with an impure heart, that work of Bernard, *De interiori domo*, chapter 50, is charged against them: *You sing in order to please the people, rather than God. You allow your voice to break, you break your will. You preserve the harmony of voices; also preserve the harmony of your conduct.* 3. If someone sings with a heart that is so composed, it cannot be otherwise than that the same person's affections are united to the song, and through it are sometimes wondrously affected. Augustine bears witness about himself; in book 9, chapter 6 of the *Confessions*, he speaks thus: *How much have I wept over your hymns and songs, how strongly moved by the voices of your sweet-sounding Church! Those voices flowed into my ears, and your truth began to flow into my heart; and from that [truth] were aroused the affections of devotion, and tears were falling, and it was well with me, with these things.* It is also worth observing what is reported about Thomas à Kempis: it is said, *While he was making music, with his face ever turned upward to heaven, inspired by divine ecstasy, doubtless captivated by the unbelievable sweetness of the psalms, he was also observed rapt beyond himself, so that sometimes he did not stay firmly with his heels on the ground, but, only touching it as far as the very tips of his toes, he contemplated flying up into heaven, where he was tending with his mind and desire, leaving his body behind,* etc. 4. Because singing serves to arouse the affections, that which is being sung ought to be understood by the one who is singing, and this is *to sing with understanding*, as we have seen above from the Apostle in 1 Corinthians 14—in Greek it is ψάλλειν τῷ νοΐ. The Apostle seems to be looking back at Psalm 47:8, where it says: *psallite*, משכיל, which although it is understood otherwise, yet the seventy elders [the Septuagint] seem to have interpreted it correctly with συνετῶς, or *intelligenter*; as if the Psalmist wanted to hint that it must

---

37. Isaiah 29:13, Matthew 15:8.
38. 1 Corinthians 14:15.

be sung thus, so that the singing might bring knowledge both to the singer and to the hearers. 5. It must especially be seen to, that we do not, out of a malignant spirit toward our enemies, add the curses which David, with God's Spirit directing him, has launched against the enemies of God (namely, Psalms 35, 69, 109), in the midst of what is to be sung. Here indeed applies the saying of Christ (Luke 9:55): *You know not of what spirit you are.* 6. Singing ought to be done with grace,[39] as the Apostle says in Colossians 3. However, indeed some understand it thus: that singing should be done with the giving of thanks, and thus the Apostle wanted to say the same thing as he had said in Ephesians 5:19. But you would have explained this more correctly, along with Theophylactus, in this way: that *in gratia* is the same thing as *cum gratia et venustate*.[40] And thus χάρις ἀντὶ χαρᾶς is understood, in chapter 4 verse 6 of this same epistle, 2 Corinthians 1:15, Ephesians 4:29, 2 Thessalonians 2:16. Also, in order that public singing in the Church might be gracious, it was provided, even in the early Church, by choirs established for this purpose. Suidas touches upon its first origin, saying as follows: *Choirs, or gatherings of singers in the Church, were divided into two parts under Constantius Constantinus, son of Marcus, and Flavianus the bishop of Antioch, singing from two places the Psalms of David. This first began at Antioch and later went out to all the ends of the world.* From this the Fathers often mention choirs of those making music. Particularly, Chrysostom in Homily 14 on 1 Timothy, where he remembers the night hymns which were accustomed to be sung[41] in the monasteries by the monks, who after being roused from sleep by their leader, stood in the church, forming the holy choir.[42] Even if this singing was publicly accepted, nevertheless it had a little more artifice. And therefore what Augustine says about Athanasius the bishop of Alexandria, in these words in Book 10, chapter 33 of the *Confessions*, might particularly please me: *That which* (he says) *I remember was often told me about the bishop of Alexandria, Athanasius, seems safer to me; for he made the lector chant the psalms with so small a variation of the voice, that it seemed closer to someone speaking than to singing. Truly, when I remember my tears which I poured forth at the singing of your church at the beginning of the recovery of my faith, even now I am moved, not by the singing, but by the things which are being sung. When they*

---

39. ἐν χάριτι.
40. With grace and beauty.
41. Reading *contari* for *cantari*.
42. τὸν ἅγιον στησάμενοι χορόν.

are sung with a clear voice and agreeable melody, I recognize again the great usefulness of this institution. Thus I fluctuate between the danger of pleasure and an experience of wholesomeness; and I am the more inclined, although not proposing indeed an irrevocable opinion, to approve of the custom of singing in the Church, so that by the delight of the ears a weaker spirit may rise to a feeling of devotion. But when it happens to me that the song moves me more than the thing which is being sung about, I confess that I have committed a sin deserving punishment, and then I would prefer not to have heard someone singing. So far Augustine. Nevertheless, the early Church appointed the psalmist, whereby grace and (if it is permitted so to speak) loveliness for Church singing could be attended to. His office was to take care that the singing proceeded agreeably and fittingly. What Baronius has in volume 1 of the *Annales Ecclesiastici*, for the year 60, should not be rejected: *But because* (he says) *the inexperience of the singers rather frequently brought it about that with a disordered sound of voices they spoiled a melodious song fitting for the Church's dignity (against whom Chrysostom rightly declaims), by necessity it was provided for in the ecclesiastical laws that no one should read in church except the singers who were appointed for this task, and those who ascend the pulpit and read from the codex.*

VIII. The musical organ can substitute for the precentor. If therefore modulated singing was accepted in the Church, and needed to be established in grace[43] with a *phonascus* or precentor leading it, and if, especially in the larger churches, he cannot be heard by everyone in accordance with the guidance which he began in order to attain the same end, then in no way will it be a sin if a musical organ, serious and not for pleasure at all, were added in order to obtain the same result. The pipe organ, also customarily played in many Reformed churches, is considered to be such a thing. The one which Jerome describes in volume 9, epistle 18 to Dardanus, seems to have been not very unlike this; he speaks about it, saying: *The hollow [part] from two elephant hides was joined together, and the bellows were compressed by twelve artisans, through fifteen bronze [or copper] pipes, into a noise great beyond measure, which shook people after the manner of thunder, so that it could be heard quite perceptibly a mile away and more, without any doubt. Thus it is proved concerning organs among the Hebrews, which are heard by their sound from Jerusalem as far as the Mount of Olives, and farther."* Those who think that Juvenal in Satire 6 was referring to organs of this type are wrong; for indeed I read these words from him [lines 379–81]: *If she enjoys singing, no*

---

43. ἐν χάριτι.

clasp[44] *belonging to anyone who sells his voice to the praetors*[45] *will hold out. Their instruments*[46] *are always in her hands; the dense [sardonyx rings on her fingers] sparkle over the entire tortoise shell [body of the instrument].*

But in no way do these agree with the organ of Jerome, much less with ours. For an ancient scholar, whoever he was, says helpfully: *He calls the* citharae *of those whom they love, organs.* Just as in the preceding lines the poet was talking about a *cithara*, so the name of organ can be appropriate for this: Isidore [of Seville] in book 3 of the *Origines* says, *"Organ" is a general term for all musical instruments. But the Greeks call by another name the one to which bellows are attached. On the other hand, it is a more popular custom of the Greeks that it be called an organ.* Nor would I think that a musical instrument completely corresponding to the modern organ had been known to the ancients, as Master Voetius has correctly judged in Thesis 1. Howsoever that may be, there is no reason meanwhile why the modern organ cannot serve to guide singing, especially in the larger churches, when otherwise there would be discord, especially if the hearers have become used to its sound and would sing confusedly without it. For if church music is thought to be suitably instituted for edification according to melodies of artistic music, and those various, and often exceedingly difficult indeed; and when Scripture itself counsels that one should sing according to grace, then truly it is consonant with reason throughout all things, that a musical instrument that contains no lasciviousness (such as our organs) may do that which can be performed less consistently and fitly by the precentor. And this is the genuine use of organs in churches, as the most noble Master Huygens has noted, who has many times criticized quite passionately their abuse, especially that accepted in churches in the Netherlands. Among Reformed theologians, Martin Bucer, the greatest man in his century, had done the same thing in his Commentary on the Psalms, edited under the name of Aretius Felinus; commenting on Psalm 33,[47] he has this,

---

44. *fibula.* The word *fibula* (brooch or clasp) is not being used here meaning a metal object used to pin together a robe. The secondary meaning is an object used for infibulation, either male or female. In the male version, a clasp, string, or even pin was used to close off the lower end of the foreskin by male singers, athletes, and performers in ancient Greece and Rome, as an indication that they were not interested in casual sexual relationships, which were sometimes expected by their fans. The next sentence's *organa* is surely a double entendre.

45. Someone hired to sing professionally on public occasions.

46. *organa.*

47. = Aretius Felinus (Martin Bucer), *Psalmorum.*

among other things: *A few years ago, the Church accepted various musical organs for the sacred hymns. But would that everyone would use them like David!—not indeed for the empty delight of the ears, but, (etc.) for calming that which disturbs the harmony of the soul, and for arousing it, whereby, more swift and fervent, kindled by devout affections, it may contemplate the loving works of God. If this is striven for, care should be taken first about the words, and truly the melody of the voices, even as of the organs, should only be adjusted for the sake of these, whereby they may be weighed more deeply and with greater ardor, both when they are heard and being spoken. Already we are letting go part of the sacred songs, while listening to melodies of the organs. However, this could have been tolerated, because meanwhile the mind excited by that melody could contemplate the holy words within itself, if that melody were so constructed as to arouse and turn toward this weighty consideration of the words. But, horrible to say, it has frequently been prevalent that church musicians, in place of holy hymns, have played tunes of extremely impure songs on the organs, by which pimps and bawds are delighted not simply with an empty pleasure, but one that is destructive at the same time; and the souls which are purer so far are lured toward lust. O wicked passivity, such that whoever has enlisted for Christ, not to mention the leaders of the Church, is not in extremely great consternation, and thoroughly frightened at these things! For in the name of Jesus Christ the Crucified, in that holy place, in the assembly of those whom he has redeemed with his own blood, for a salary which is paid on behalf of his worship, nothing else is done but sacrificing to Venus; the chaste hearts and minds of the saints are being desecrated, and those who are utterly lost are being titillated.* Thus far Bucer.

IX. That nevertheless it is not absolutely necessary. Nevertheless, I will not argue that it is necessary that there should be organs in churches. For where the people have grown accustomed to sing without them, and not sing miserably, they can be spared the expense since more than ordinary funds are required to be disbursed both for the musical instrument and for the one who plays it. Indeed, it seems discordant to me that the work of some musician, just because he knows how to play the organ skillfully, should be remunerated with a greater salary than that of a minister of the Divine Word, learned and pious in other respects. I will leave the use of the organ as *adiaphorus*, having followed the judgment in article 50 of the venerable Synod of South Holland held in Delft in the year 1638. For the rest, wherever an organ is already established in a church, it is completely wicked to misuse it. The most noble Master Huygens has noted various abuses, some of them very great, in his little book which has been praised several times. But it is shameful to present profane melodies, inasmuch as they serve to arouse carnal pleasure. Nor is it to be endured, that there should be playing for a secular purpose when the holy assembly is being dismissed. Zepper himself is indignant on that account in book 4, chapter 9 of *De lege Mosaica*,[48] and also is quoted by the author of the *Damascus Altar* on page 494. *In certain Reformed churches* (he says) *those organs are still retained, but they are not played for secular uses unless all portions of divine worship have been completed, and the church congregation has been dismissed, on account of those who seek some delight from this sound and the harmonies, and to whom it is pleasing to be involved in this instrumental music.* Indeed, I confess that no sanctity belongs to our churches in themselves; but in the meantime, since they are devoted to holy use, and Christians may appear in them to perform their reasonable worship, they should not be devoted to secular uses, nor even, unless perhaps necessity constrains it, to civil uses. Thus far I approve what Bernard has in his sermon 5 on the dedication of a church; he is quoted also by Master Huygens: *What holiness* (he says) *do these stones have? Undoubtedly they have holiness, but on account of your bodies. Can anyone really doubt that your bodies are holy, which are the temple of the Holy Spirit, so that each one may know how to possess his own vessel in holiness? Because the Spirit of God is dwelling in you, therefore your souls are holy: your bodies are holy on account of your souls; and even the house is holy on account of your bodies.* And so it is not to be borne at all that the church is transformed into a club[49] (so the Greeks are accustomed to call a place into which idle people come together for the sake of conversation), and that the pleasures of the organ are displayed to thieves (if not those who do worse things), when it is not indeed playing sacred songs, but often profane, if not also base, ones. If a church has an organ, the person put in charge of it should be an experienced guide, and certainly it cannot be devoted to a more appropriate use than to guide the singing of the church congregation. And so the arrangement at the church in Leiden should not be criticized, which not so many years ago required the organs to play the psalms and praises of God; any less sacred use was taken away. However, I would not advocate that an organ be introduced (where the people are used to singing knowledgeably); lest it be thought that there is no other attention and devotion of those singing except insofar as it is directed by an

---

48. Zepper, *Legum Mosaicarum*, 346ff.
49. λέσχιω.

inanimate instrument. This very thing I say again, I repeat, because I feared the malicious teeth of envy. I consider this our opinion, elaborated thus far, to be so fair and moderate that a more accommodating one certainly could not be thought of, by reason of a thing being *adiaphora* in itself.

X. Responding to those arguments of Master Voetius that he himself calls "direct." Furthermore, we will have accomplished nothing up to this point unless we likewise answer the arguments of Master Voetius. These are not only measured out to the unsuspecting reader by the handful, but by the peck, indeed by the bushel. And in order that they may appear more formidable, he draws them up in a line of battle, distributed as it were into legions.[50] For I will count the direct arguments, the arguments which are indirect and derived from absurd consequences, likewise the arguments which are indirect and *ad hominem*, and the authorities. Therefore: Direct Argument 1, occurring in Thesis 4, is this: *Christ and the apostles, or the apostolic church, did not use such music, nor did they teach the use of it in order to bring greater devotion or some sort of perfection to worship in church.* Answer: But for an equal reason the reverend gentleman might conclude that the Church should not have church buildings, or at least those which were consecrated by a Papist ritual; for the Church not only did without them in the time of the apostles, but for some centuries after. So far it is certain that Christians were more conspicuous for sincere devotion and deeply imbued by piety in the time when they were forming their gatherings, whether in private homes or even in caves. By reason of the external rites of the Church, Christ left to us this general rule through the apostle Paul, in the last verse [40] of 1 Corinthians 14: *Let everything be done decently and in good order.*[51] However, certain orthodox churches have judged it suitable that the pipe organ guide the singing. What sin is here? Argument II is set forth in these words: *Because it not only does not arouse, increase and confirm the soul's spiritual and reasonable devotion and worship, but on the contrary it impedes, breaks, scatters, softens, and weakens these, while by those imperceptible things it leads astray, toward perceptible and lower pleasures, the powers and intention of the soul.* Answer: This is conceded concerning that music which is weak and very artificial, which is performed in the Popish domain with various musical instruments added;

50. Interestingly, Schoock here uses the word *manipulus*, which can mean both a *handful*, or a miliary unit of sixty to 120 men: he's treating Voetius's arguments as soldiers to fight.

51. In this citation of 1 Corinthians 14:40 Schoock does not include *in the house of the Lord*.

but indeed in no way is there a concession about that music which the organ produces, with sober modulation according to the singing. Cajetan, whose authority the reverend gentleman boasted about thereafter, had spoken about it only once. Argument III is this: *Even if it were a most excellent thing in itself, anything in public worship that neither edifies nor is suitable for edifying the church should not be used. But organ music is such a thing; therefore, the major* [premise] *is proved by 1 Corinthians 14: 12, 16, 17, 19, and 26. The minor* [premise] *is proved, because while the organ is sounding either alone or antiphonally, the Church does not understand either the polyphonic modulation or the sacred words for which that harmony is called suitable, and consequently she cannot say "Amen."* Answer: We absolutely admit the major premise, but not equally the minor, even though it combats the Papists who produce excessively luxuriant singing with the choirs who sing in their churches, and meanwhile the people are silent. But this cannot be applied to the organ, about which we are talking here, for that guides the voices of singers. So, if it is permitted in the assembly of the faithful to sing psalms with skill, why cannot the organ set forth the melodies to be held onto during the singing as a favor to those untrained and inexperienced in music? Also, as it is established that devotion is not disturbed by the unaccompanied voices of singers, then, if during the singing they stay with the musical melodies by the prescription of their art, thus likewise it can be judged that in no way will it disturb the devotion of the mingled crowd, when the organ, going ahead, shows it how the singing should be properly presented according to the laws of instrumental music. If the proposition that the reverend gentleman cites for his minor premise should be permitted without reserve, then the singing commanded by God himself through David ought not to be retained. Whatever even the reverend gentleman supposes, I hardly think that Bernard was wrong when he wrote thus in *A Book for a Sister on the Way of Living Well*:[52] *However hard are the hearts of worldly human beings, as soon as they hear the sweetness of the psalms, they are converted to the love of piety. There are many who, pierced by the delightfulness of the psalms, lament their sins.* Argument IV is presented thus: *Whatever is a fertile occasion of many evils, and liable to many abuses, should not be employed in public worship, if indeed it might be* adiaphorum, *or at least, in itself, might not be necessary or very useful; but such is the music of the organ.* Answer: But therefore why is something being overlooked about such enormous abuses of the organ?—since indeed, among the Reformed

---

52. = Bernard of Clairvaux 1090–1153), *Liber de modo*, 184: cols. 1199–1306.

themselves, in a church dedicated to holy activities, it is generally supposed to serve to delight people of this world, while they are walking around, or even at the same time as they are heedlessly talking about the things of this world. Abuses which can easily be guarded against beforehand cannot, for any reason, take something away from the legitimate use of anything.

XI. Meeting the "indirect" arguments of Master Voetius. There follows the second battleline of the reverend gentleman, comprising his indirect arguments drawn from absurd consequences, which include the following: [Argument] I. *Because it smells of Judaism, or of the peculiar, immature, and organized worship of the Old Testament; and by the same rule, Aaron's bells (Exodus 28:34-35), the silver trumpets of the priests (Numbers 10:2-3), the horns of Joel (Leviticus 25:9), the* citharae, nablia, cymbala, *along with the Levite singers (1 Chronicles 25: 1, 6) and so the entire organized worship, could be introduced in the New Testament churches.* Answer 1: It must be properly noted that God did not by any means prescribe the use of instrumental music through Moses, who nevertheless received the ceremonial law, but that David introduced it by a special command of God, as we have seen earlier. [Answer] 2: I would certainly think that the people of Israel in the time of Moses, and also in the time of David, were living more in the age of childhood; and so the eminent gentleman is acting in vain when he makes comments on the childish worship of the Israelites. [Answer] 3: Whatever had been observed by the Israelites concerning the sacred worship was not equally abrogated, but insofar and to the extent that they were types [of things fulfilled in the New Testament]. Otherwise you might equally infer that it is not right for Christians to have church buildings, or suspended candelabra for use at nighttime services. Those things which serve for the convenience of holy activity must be considered as common to the Israelites and to Christians. [Argument] II. The reasoning is contained in these words: *Because it is a poor imitation*[53] *of the gentiles, and belongs with their worship. That is absurd. For just as the gentiles commingled games and spectacles with their solemnities and sacred rites, so also they commingled music.* Answer 1: The same objection could be made about David too. Answer 2: As the devil loves to be the ape of God, so he prescribed to the gentiles various rituals, often with ridiculous additions, to be observed by them as if in holy rites; because they [rituals] had been ordained by God himself, whom the devil hoped that he could put to shame for this reason. Answer 3: Not everything which the gentiles did must then be rejected, since indeed they

---

53. κακοζηλία.

did many things by the prescription of natural law, which is a good gift of God. Answer 4: But those things which are linked either with the profanation of God or with the lewdness of the flesh should not be done according to the example of the gentiles. Peter also teaches this when in his first letter, chapter 4, verse 3, he speaks thus: *It is enough for you that, in past life, you committed those things which were pleasing to gentiles: walking in licentiousness, desires, drunkenness, feasting, carousing, and wicked worship of idols.* [Argument] III. The reverend gentleman proceeds thus: *It would follow that also many other things, which the senses can perceive, and which are carnal, should be introduced into public worship, for the sake of some carnal or ignorant people who are affected by these things; dancing (of course), theater, games, and any delights whatsoever of the ears and eyes.* Answer 1: It does not follow; and already beforehand we have precisely stipulated that the singing should not serve to soothe the ears for any reason. Answer 2: Now if, by reason of the musical melodies (which is very well known), many psalms in the Netherlands' churches are sung to tunes of songs which otherwise are secular, why cannot the organ direct those melodies (lest the singing become discordant)? For either artistic melodies should be absent from the psalms (especially such as those) or the organ can also lead such melodies. [Argument] IV. He says: *It would follow that the Church, both the apostolic one and the ancient one throughout so many centuries, was less devout, or at least less attentive to stirring up the devotion of their listeners, especially of the more ignorant and weaker sort.* Answer 1: This should have been thought of: that the primitive apostolic Church groaned for a long time under the cross, nor could it have been able to make use of everything for the exercise of public worship, on account of the persecutions. For this reason it also lacked church buildings for a long time, which in the subsequent centuries were erected according to religious usage and order; thus they, even up to this present time, also serve the appropriate use of the orthodox churches. Answer 2: By the same reasoning, the reverend gentleman contends that the Latin Church was disgraced by Ambrose, when he introduced antiphonal singing, as Augustine himself hints in the *Confessions*, book 9, chapter 7; and also that the devotion of the Greek churches had grown sluggish long before, if indeed Ambrose received this singing from them, which Basil the Great also remembers in his Letter 63. Answer 3: Indeed, I should think that the organ, serving the plain singing of the church congregation by its guidance, should be accepted rather than antiphons. [Argument] V: The reverend gentleman proceeds thus: *It would follow that the public or ecclesiastical exercises of piety (among which is doxology, or praise of God through psalms and hymns) are able to take place apart from the Church, and to be restricted to some definite people specially assigned and consecrated for that purpose: obviously, organists and the wind instrument players currently associated with them, and musicians or choir boys.* Answer 1: It is astonishing that a serious theologian is being so foolish about consequences. By the same reasoning, he might conclude that the exercises of public devotion can be restricted to the lectors and cantors, whom thus far he himself has not yet taught the Church to exterminate. Answer 2: By our hypothesis (which is equally that of the most noble Master Huygens), an organist with his organ, in holy exercises and those in public, is intended to assist the cantor in guiding the song of the whole church congregation. If the precentor is employed rightfully for the guidance of singing, then truly the organist also can be employed appropriately. [Argument] VI. Master Voetius argues thus from the absurd, as it were: *It would follow, that because of carnal and more ignorant people, the universal Church would be deprived, for such a great span of time, of the most noblest and most excellent method for leading people to God, which is through preaching, reading, prayer, intelligible and shared psalmody. But it is absurd for precious hours of public gatherings to be wasted by these* [other] *things, and for souls to be sent out starving on nothing but bran, or inflated by bellows and wind, instead of having been fed.* Answer 1: It is astonishing that the learned gentleman puts the abuse of the organ in the same place as the legitimate use, on behalf of which we are writing and disputing so far. Answer 2: Those things which Erasmus, and others who were called upon for their opinion by the reverend gentleman, censured in the Papists, we have discussed with the greatest fairness. Answer 3: If the organ, serving for the guidance of regular singing, may be employed by the reasoning which we have already indicated before, not even Momus[54] would discover anything which he could reasonably accuse.

XII. Testing Master Voetius's self-styled "ad hominem" arguments. There follows in the reverend gentleman's discussion a third category of arguments, comprising those which are indirect or (as he calls them) κατ ἄνθρωπον, or *ad hominem*. It is appropriate to review this [category] also; as the reverend gentleman has indeed gathered his skirmishers here, so it must be seen whether these can do more than his reserve ranks, who have already been repulsed. Therefore [argument] I proceeds thus: *The fantasy*

---

54. The Greek god of mockery and censure.

and complexity[55] *of instrumental sound are repugnant to simplicity, to a spiritual turning inward, to withdrawing, and to laying bare the heart, and to elevation away from external and corporeal things, which various people have commended to the devout so greatly.* Answer 1: But by the same reason, the reverend gentleman might argue against those who sing with unaccompanied voices, and that our Psalter should divest itself of musical melodies. If these [melodies] are legitimately used, and those who sing in the church, in order to avoid confusion, ought to join their voices in accordance with them to guard in advance against confusion, then the organ can also be employed properly and in order; indeed by its assistance the people, and those who are inexperienced in music, will be helped so that they can sing without confusion. Answer 2: Because it smells of art (against[56] rhetoric or music), in the next place it does not serve to disturb the attention and devotion of the mind; the Holy Spirit himself shows that a pious heart can join devotion with art, through Job and various prophets, by speaking allegorically in many places, and in language that is quite figurative. Indirect Argument II is this: *By taking over vocal and intelligible singing, it is repugnant to simplicity and to the cautious moderation of the ancient Church, which was so great that even at the time of Augustine, there were Western bishops who would not allow any singing.* Answer 1: I doubt that what the reverend gentleman has asserted, as it were, about the time of Augustine could be proved out of Augustine or any other ancient writer. The reverend gentleman cites Pichius but that one is not at hand, and I fear that he [Voetius] is being deceitful. Answer 2: But granted that certain churches did reject public singing, and still reject it (for we have abundantly proved in section III above that in the New Testament it was not commended for public use), what is gained by this? For I would not think that the reverend gentleman wants to infer by this, that singing in the churches should be abolished. Answer 3: Also, if he permits the use of singing which is artistic in its melody, why does he not equally permit the organ, which guides the artistic melodies as a help to the less trained? [Argument] III. He says, *It is repugnant to the simplicity of singing. Even as the ancients, so also the popes themselves did not want singing to be decorated either with division* [ornamentation] *or harmonic multiplicity of voices, so that people would thus be drawn away from being attentive.* Answer 1: None of the ancients has utterly condemned artistic singing, but that which corresponds to theatrical

---

55. πολυποιχιλία.

56. V.C. = *vide contra*. V.C. is frequently employed to redirect readers toward an opposing viewpoint or argument.

music (as we have seen above, nor do the authors whom the reverend gentleman has cited himself teach something else). Answer 2: If this argument of the renowned gentleman should be valid, at the same time he should take out the artistic melodies from the Psalter, and order anyone in the church congregation to sing in his own way and with his own melodies. [Argument] IV. *Because* (he says), *as the* Caeremoniale Episcoporum *book 1 chapter 23 decrees, other musical instruments should not be used in the Church. So, by the same reason, neither organs nor ornamented organ music [should be used].* Answer 1: But this consequence does not follow from the same reason in any way. For the organ has nothing lascivious about it, so it cannot be listed in the same place as other musical instruments. Answer 2: After other musical instruments were cast out so that there would be nothing lascivious in sacred singing, the organ began to be used frequently; the Papists equally commend it, and a considerable number of our churches use it. [Argument] V. And finally Master Voetius attacks his adversaries thus: *For they do not adhere to that antiquity which must be venerated, which nevertheless they pretend everywhere that they still desire to do; but clearly, for their part, they prefer innovations and Greek frivolities to ancient and serious devotion.* And then he discourses copiously about the first origins of the organ. Answer 1: I willingly concede that the organ was an invention of the Greeks; but why is it accused of frivolity because of that? By the same reasoning you would reject all philosophy as "a collection of Greeklings."[57] [Answer] 2: The organ was wisely thought of lest some levity be noted in Church singing. [Answer] 3: Churches began to be built later by Christians; therefore Master Voetius may conclude that they should be destroyed. [Answer] 4: With respect to those things which, in the manner of furniture, are serviceable for church use, often they can obtain an advantage through innovation. This should particularly be noted concerning the organ. [Answer] 5: Given—from [the life of] Vitalian, to be exact—that around the year of our Christ 770, the use of the organ had been sought for Western churches; what other point would the reverend gentleman win from this, but that human industry thought later of a musical instrument which could serve conveniently to guide the singing of the Church? When Balthasar Lydius the Elder,[58] minister of the

---

57. ὀύρημα Graeculorum.

58. = Balthasar Lydius (1577–1629), a Reformed minister in Dordrecht from 1602 until his death in 1629. He was delegated by the Synod of South Holland to attend the international synod of Dordrecht, and as the local pastor two honors fell to him: he preached the opening sermon (in Dutch) on November 13, 1618, and he offered the opening prayer (in Latin) for first session of the Synod.

church at Dordrecht while he was alive, a learned man and possessor of a most erudite library, brought out in Dutch the treatise of Franciscus Alaers, *De traditionibus ecclesiae Romanae*, with annotations, he provides these notes with a plea about the organs, as if introduced by Vitalian: *Concerning organs in churches, we know very well that God can also be thanked by means of musical instruments, according to countless passages in holy Scripture. But care has to be taken that nothing else but spiritual songs of praise be played on it, and that with solemn music, and not with such frivolous, bouncy dance music that feet start tapping because of it,*[59] *where only the Spirit of God should be received, with a godly joy.* What can be said equally according to our judgment? Also, this Lydius, as long as he was permitted by fate, cherished a very close relationship with Master Voetius. Therefore there is no reason why the authority of this same man should not also be admitted by the other.

XIII. To what extent the decisions of certain Dutch synods support Master Voetius. Finally, the reverend gentleman, in his customary manner, argues from authority. But we have already considered beforehand to what degree the authors whom he cites support him. He seems to have greater support in certain decisions of Dutch synods, especially in canon 50 of the Synod of Dordtrecht held in 1574, and in the response to question 34 of the Synod of Middelburg held in 1581. But I am little moved by these. [Answer 1.] First, indeed, I answer that in the said synods certain things were decreed which are unanimously condemned by most churches in the United Netherlands today. As the Church was new, not yet stabilized, and exposed to danger from the many calumnies and plots of her enemies, many things were unacceptable for a time, which afterward were accepted usefully and for edification. Specifically the Synod of Dordtrecht condemns in canon 24 the laying on of hands for the ordination of new ministers; in canon 42, ministers' prayers that depart from the accustomed liturgy; in canon 51, evening meetings; in canon 55, visitors of the sick who were not ministers of the Church; in canon 64, the threefold immersion in baptism; and in canon 75 it contends that the Lord's Supper should be received while standing rather than seated. The same can be supposed about organs; just as, due to the circumstances of the time, it was acceptable to remove them from the churches, so afterwards other synods in the Netherlands (as we have seen above) have consented to them as *adiaphora*. [Answer] 2. If everything is diligently weighed, it will be clear that it was acceptable to remove organs on account of abuse. For canon 50 of the said Synod has this: *Concerning organ playing in the congregations,*

---

59. dat de voeten daer licht van worden.

some think it ought to be entirely done away with, following Paul's teaching in 1 Corinthians 14:19. And although it [the organ] is still used in some of these churches at the end of the service when the people are leaving, it mostly serves to make the people forget what they have just heard, and we need to worry that afterwards it will be used for superstition, just as it now serves for frivolity. And if this were to be discontinued, it would be easier to collect the offerings at the door when the people are leaving, rather than to do so in the middle of the service, at which time it greatly disrupts the worship of God. We, and Master Huygens before us, equally condemn what the Synod condemns here. If he had been in agreement with the Synod concerning a more appropriate use of organs, without a doubt it would have commended the same use. Meanwhile, "the day teaches the day."[60] [Answer] 3. Someone could think that, in order for this fiftieth canon against organs to be produced, some people prevailed with their votes against their fellow ministers[61] in the synodical session. At the same time they lacked organs in their churches, and perhaps (God knows!) they were envious of the rest of their colleagues for the use of these; indeed, pastors themselves are only human. The eldest of the pastors at Bremen, Johannes Capito, was well-known, a man learned in other respects, zealous, and pious. He had pastored the orthodox church at Bruges, in Flanders, at the same time when Cornelius Adriani, the Franciscan of celebrated name, who lived at Dordt, was exercising his abusive[62] eloquence. Now this Capito, since he did not have an organ in his church, Saint Martin's [in Bremen], where he ordinarily taught, habitually railed against it with daily invective, to the point of calling the Cornemuse[63] the devil's pipe. But when by the generosity of the Senate an organ was installed in his church too, he could not find praises worthy of it, and now called it the music of angels, a foretaste of the joy of heaven, and who knows what else. Thus do the judgments of men often change as the times change. However, I do not bring this forward for this reason, as though I would enjoy troubling the departed spirit of a venerable old man, but because I considered that this story, which I know is altogether true, would not be foreign to my purpose. And so much for organs.

---

60. A well-known proverb of Schoock's time; like the modern phrase *live and learn*.
61. *symmistae*.
62. Literally, "canine eloquence."
63. The name of an organ stop that is meant to sound like bagpipes.

GILBERTUS VOETIUS, ANDREAS ESSENIUS, AND MATTHIAS NETHENUS

Theological Advice (1655)

Voetius was not done writing about the organ when he finished the essay for Politicæ ecclesisticæ, nor did his anti-orgelist position waver. For example, joined by University of Utrecht colleagues Andreas Essenius (1618–1677) and Matthias Nethenus (1618–1686), he issued yet another condemnation of all organ use in public worship in 1655. This triumvirate of anti-orgelists must have savored the opportunity to have a chance to silence Utrecht's church organs once and for all when the city council requested the professors's advice to answer the question "Whether the Christian Civic Authorities have the power, during this time of the New Testament, to institute the playing of the organ during the public singing of the psalms, all the more and principally since this had not been the custom previously."[1] The trio eagerly accepted "such an honest request." The authors concluded that a Christian government that did not wish to exceed the bounds of its duties could not and should not introduce organ playing during the public singing of the psalms.

---

1. *Of de Christelike Overheyd ten tijde des Nieuwen Testamentz vermoegende het speelen van den Orgel onder het openbaare Psalmsinghen in de kercekn in te voeren, te meer en voornamelick als sulks te vooren in geen gebruyck is geweest.*

1 | PROFESSORS

Maarten Albert Vente and C. C. Vlam, eds. *Documentaet et archivalia ad historiam musicæ neerlandicæ. Bouwstenen voor een geschiedenis der toonkunst in de Nederlanden.* Amsterdam: Vereniging voor Nederlandse muziekgeschiedenis, 1965, 234–5.

Utrecht, Archief der Hervormde Gemeente, *Afdeling Kerkeraad I*

(bijlage bij de notulen van de Kerkeraad d.d. 31 october 1683)

Utrecht, Archives of the Reformed Congregation

Section Consistory I
(addendum to the minutes of the Consistory, dated October 31, 1683)

January 29, 1655

THEOLOGICAL ADVICE

We the undersigned professors of Sacred Theology at the Academy of Utrecht, having been requested to express our feelings concerning the following question: Whether the Christian Authorities in the age of the New Testament are able to institute the playing of the organ during the public singing of the Psalms in the churches, all the more and mainly because this had not been the custom in the past? [We] did not want to or could not decline such an honest request and therefore answer the above-mentioned question in this manner:

In the first place we understand that the making of rules how the singing in the churches, being a part of the public worship service, should be done and directed is a purely ecclesiastical (church) affair, and therefore should made by the church, by the leaders of the congregation that have been appointed for that task. Secondly, even though music is an honorable practice, and outside the public worship service, in private or in public places may be used for pleasant entertainment, and ought to be used to play psalms and spiritual songs. But just the same, the playing of the organ in the public worship of the New Testament is a useless and unedifying practice, which draws the thoughts of the majority of the Christians from appropriate attention toward human entertainment, and thus prevents rather than promotes true worship, which must happen in spirit and in truth. Note then that the apostle teaches us in which way we should conduct the meetings of the believers and to which end all public acts and practices that are carried out there should be directed, when he writes this way in 1 Corinthians 14:26 to the Corinthians: *How is it then brothers? When you meet together, does each of you have a psalm, does he have a teaching, does he have a (foreign) language, does he have a revelation, does he have an explanation: let all things be done to edify.* The apostle, therefore, desires that in all things we shall consider the edification of the whole congregation. But as there is no inherent ability in the organ playing to a general edification and stimulation of the congregation of the Lord toward spiritual attention, but it is a dumb and nonsensical (unreasonable) noise about which no one can say anything else. 1 Corinthians 14:16. About which Christ, his apostles, the apostolic and succeeding ancient churches had no knowledge. Which, however, from the Jewish religion, in which Christ and his disciples grew up, could have introduced some musical instruments and playing into the Christian worship service of the New Testament, if they had thought that appropriate for general edification.

We judge, therefore, that the Christian authorities, which do not wish to exceed the boundaries of their calling and which earnestly seek the promotion of the kingdom of Christ and the true spiritual religion of the Christians, are hereby being notified, that they may not under any circumstances introduce the playing of the organ during the public singing of the Psalms. Even more so, as this has not been and is not a custom from earlier time.

As proclamation of the truth we have put our personal signatures below this our opinion. Dated at Utrecht in the year 1655 of January 29.

Gisbertus Voetius, Andreas Essenius, Matthias Nethenus

2
People

JEAN-ETIENNE DURANTI

De ritibus Ecclesiae cath[olicae], chapter XIII: *De organis* (1591)

Jean-Etienne Durand (1534–1589) was a French magistrate and the first president at the Parliament of Toulouse. He was also a devout Roman Catholic who opposed the Huguenots. But his loyalty to Henry III led to his arrest by the orders of the Catholic League, who mistrusted him. He was shot to death by a member of the League in 1589. Most of his works, like this one, were published posthumously.

**Jean-Etienne Duranti, *De ritibus Ecclesiae cath*[*olicae*], chapter XIII: *De organis*.
Romæ: Ex Typographia Vaticana, 1591, 69ff:**

Chapter 13: Concerning Organs

1. What an organ is, and the various types of organs.
2. *The use of organs in the Church is very ancient, even though it is not so certain [that it was] from the first beginning.*
3. *The correct use of organs is described, and the abuse is censured.*

1. The organ is called a musical instrument by the authority of Augustine [in his commentary] on Psalm 56: not only one which is large and inflated by bellows, but indeed whatever is adapted to melody, and is a physical

object.[1] Isidore [of Seville] says, in book 3 chapter 20 of the *Origine*,[2] that *organum* is a general term for all musical apparatus, but that the Greeks call by a different name the one to which bellows are attached. However, it is a more common custom to call it *organum*. There are various types of musical organs. Some are stretched with strings; these are called *cruomena* ["bags"], or *enchorda* ["strung in"], or *entata* ["stretched things"]. Some are inflated by the breath, others by machine. Those which are water-driven are *hydraulica*. And there are several others, about which Caelius Rhodiginus,[3] in book 9 chapter 6 of *Lect[iones] antiqua[e]* says: *Therefore, that which is written in Psalm 150, "Praise him with strings and organ," is not understood to be about organs which are blown with bellows.* Amalar[ius] Fortunatus has also pointed this out in book 3 chapter 3 of *On Ecclesiastical Offices*. There is more about organs in Saint Jerome's *Epistula 28 ad Dardanum*, and Isidore's *Origines*, book 3, chapters 19, 20, and 21.

2. Julianus, [commenting] on Job chapter 31, proves that the use of organs in places of worship was very ancient, citing those words: *But if I have walked with the scoffers, or with vanity*, with these words: *Indeed the situation is far otherwise: for the use of organs was not forbidden, seeing that this very thing could be done with piety. For they themselves used them in houses of worship.* But this Julianus came a long time before Saint Gregory. For the rest, it is doubtful who first discovered the organs which we use today. Glicas[4] and Manasses,[5] writing on the Emperor Theophilus, attribute the invention of organs to Theophilus. But the authorities who say that the use of organs was accepted in the Church long before Theophilus, when Vitalian was pope, are: Martin Pollonus,[6] Platina Ioannettus, and several others, out of the [*Liber*] *Pontificalis* of Pope Damasus. Marianus Scotus, an authority on Pepin, says that organs were sent to King Pepin [III] by Constantine [V] the Greek emperor. Also the monk Aimoin affirms, in book 4 chapter 113 of *De gestis Francorum*, that organs of the Greek type were first

---

1. *Enarrationes in psalmos* (56:16): Organa *dicuntur omnia instrumenta musicorum. Non solum illud organum dicitur, quod grande est, et inflatur follibus; sed quidquid aptatur ad cantilenam, et corporeum est, quo instrumento utitur qui cantat,* organum *dicitur.* We call all musical instruments *organ*. Not only the great organ with wind pipes, but any tool that can produce a tune, has a body, and can be used by a singer is called *organum*.

2. alternate name for the *Etymologiae*.

3. = Lodovico Ricchieri (1469–1525).

4. = Michael Glycas (12th c).

5. = Constantine Manasses (c.1130–c.1187).

6. = Martin of Opava (d. 1278).

built in France by the skill of a certain man named Gregory, during the reign of Louis the Pious, at his expense. Therefore this will not be in agreement with Navarro, for in chapter 16 of the book *De oratione et horis canonicis*, he has written repeatedly that the use of organs had not yet been accepted, according to the testimony of Saint Thomas Aquinas. Clearly, although the use of organs is not necessary, since organs do not exist in the papal chapel, as Cajetan on Saint Thomas [in his commentary on the *Summa Theologica*] and Sotus,[7] in book 10, question 5, article 2 of *De just[icia] et jure*, bear witness, nevertheless Saint Thomas in 2. 2. question 91 and Scotus, as cited above, should not be rejected. For countless passages of holy Scripture have stated that God should be praised with flutes, timbrels, and other musical instruments.

3. Democares asserts fully in chapter 14 of *De observanda missarum celebratione* that the Synod of Sens in chapter 17 accepted the use of organs in the Church by the fathers for worship and divine service, except that the organs should play nothing except sacred hymns and spiritual songs. Likewise, at the Council of Cologne: *Let the melody of organs be employed in churches in this way: that it should not arouse wantonness rather than devotion, nor should anything be played besides sacred hymns and spiritual songs.* This was repeated in the diocesan Synod of Augsburg, and the Synod of Trent in session 22 concerning the things to be observed and to be avoided in the celebration of the Mass, with these words: *And let them exclude from the churches those types of music, whether for organ or voice, with which anything lascivious or impure is mingled*, etc.

---

7. = Domingo de Soto (1494–1560).

COUNCIL OF SNEEK

Terms and Conditions for a new Organist (1602)

The magistrates of Sneek, a prominent city in the province of Friesland, were concerned not only about their pipe organs, but also about the persons who played them. The Resolutions *were as clear as they were demanding: the organ would only be used in a holy manner to play solemn music. To do so, the player of the organ must be equally solemn and holy—even committing never to perform music in a pub. This record reiterates the strong hold Dutch city councils had on their pipe organs, organists, and churches.*

Oud Archief Sneek invoice number 1. *Resolutieboek Sneek,* 1580–1663, folio 42:[1]

17 April 1602

2) Terms and conditions under which the burgomasters, sheriffs, and council men of the city of Sneek intend to appoint and hire a good organist. In the first place, the organist will be responsible at all times to maintain the Great Organ in the Great Church, and the small one in the Orphan's Church, so that these instruments will sound well and with resonance, all this at his own cost. And when the organist shall leave the aforesaid instruments, either by resignation or by request to leave, he shall be bound to hand over these organs in good and proper state, as indicated above.

---

1. I thank Mr. H. Jaasma, archivist of the City Archive of Sneek, for his assistance in locating this document.

COUNCIL OF SNEEK | TERMS AND CONDITIONS

The organist will never play secular[2] songs in the aforementioned churches but only spiritual psalms and hymns. The organist will play on all preaching days, both on Sundays and through the week, for half an hour before the service and half an hour after the service, in both churches. And if the aforementioned council would instruct him at any time to play for an hour at the aforementioned times, he will be bound to do so. The same organist will also be bound to play from five until six in the evening throughout the year whenever it pleases the council. The organist will also never play in any pub or other place, and there play secular[3] songs. And the aforementioned council as well as the organist may give each other notice to discontinue the employment, a quarter of a year before the end of the year. On this date, 17 April 1602 the council has agreed with Mr. Harmen Jansen, organist, that he will play both of the organs from the first of May next till the first of May in the next year 1603 in accordance with the rules above, and that for the time mentioned he will receive the sum of one hundred and sixty carolus guilders, each consisting of twenty stuivers as his salary and each will receive a quarter of this money each quarter of the year. By these present, signed by the hand of the secretary to the Council and by Mr. Harmen signed below himself.

2. *lichtvaerdige*.
3. *lichtvaerdige*.

JAN JANSZ. CALCKMAN

Antidotum (excerpt, 1641)

Though a layperson, Jan Jansz. Calckman had no problem publishing his theological views. Sound Theology reviews in detail his colorful career and the circumstances that caused him to published Antidotum, *a reactionary work against Huygens's* Orgel Gebruyck,[1] *and reviews Calckman's four principle objections to organ use. What follows here is an additional excerpt that comes near the end of Calckman's work. The references* you, your, Orgelist, *and* Organ-Builder *are directed at Huygens. After publishing this work, Calckman was put under censure by his consistory (even as they began an investigation into the accomplice printer, Aert van Meurs), and denied the sacrament of communion until he apologized. Calckman did so, two weeks later, "with tears."*

Antidotum, tegen-gift vant gebruyck of on-gebruyck vant orgel inde kercken der Vereenighde Nederlanden. 's-Gravenhage: Aert van Meurs, 1641, 193ff:

That you speak so disparagingly about all simple members [of the church] and others, saying *Their singing sounds like birds of different beaks, and the music is in conflict like clashing pails used to get water from a well.* The sounds made by your organ-builder sound much more dissonant than

---

1. For an excellent English translation, see *Use and Non-Use of the Organ in the Churches of the United Netherlands*, translated by Erika E. Smit-van Rotte, New York: Institute of Mediæval Music, 1964.

birds of a different kind [singing together], so that the music fights more with each other than clanging wash tubs. And I will prove that to you even if you don't want to believe it! For who exceeds the boundaries of the music more than those who do not speak when the word of God speaks (1 Peter 4:11[2])? Where you should have proved your case from God's word, instead you draw another register [organ stop], whose tone[3] is in total contrast [to God's word]; that is, the heathen feelings of worldly music placing God's word opposite the darkness, the truth against the lie, attempting to seek the good in the evil. *Wine grapes* [growing] *on the thorns, and figs on the thistles* (Matthew 7:26[4]). Observe, Organ-Builder, how dissonant those [organ] sounds mix through each other and attempt to *compare God with Belial* (2 Corinthians 6:15[5]) and begin to sing the song of the heathens and others who have no knowledge of the true religion but sing as they had been taught, like the birds. Those voices mingle with yours (take heed!) *that the music should war with each other more than scooping-pails,*[6] But you go far beyond the measure of God's Word when you judge the congregation about its singing. God does not judge the congregation by voice but by the heart, even if they did not sing. God has not set a measure or standard for the congregation in comparison to worldly singers but according to the measure of the Spirit. A singer gives to God in simplicity what he has received from God. If the music then conflicts with worldly music, it does not conflict with the measure of the Spirit. Thus, "Orgelist," you seek to remove simple singing from the congregation [by] introducing the use of the organ, about which the majority of the congregation knows as much as a cow in Flanders. Therefore consider carefully what service you render to God, and what benefit you bring to the Christian congregation. You speak so disparagingly of the congregation's worship, saying their singing is all yelling and screaming, the one high, the other low, and other offenses.

    2. *If anyone speaks, they should do so as one who speaks the very words of God. If anyone serves, they should do so with the strength God provides, so that in all things God may be praised through Jesus Christ. To him be the glory and the power for ever and ever. Amen.*

    3. Calckman here plays on organ terms *draw*, *register* (an organ stop), *tone*.

    4. *But everyone who hears these words of mine and does not put them into practice is like a foolish man who built his house on sand.* But surely a typographical error: It is Matthew 7:16 that says: *By their fruit you will recognize them. Do people pick grapes from thornbushes, or figs from thistles?*

    5. *What harmony is there between Christ and Belial? Or what does a believer have in common with an unbeliever?*

    6. Pails used to empty latrines.

2 | PEOPLE

And then you dare say: People surely would not tolerate that simpleton to do anything in matters of minor importance, let alone what is done before the face of God. This is nothing less than betraying Christ with a kiss (Luke 22:48) and in the meantime taking away the singing from the church by introducing the heathen organ for the worship of God!

ABCOUDE

Request to magistrates to cease organ music in the churches (1649)

Municipal proclamations did not always change the minds in the pew or church council room. This communication from the church council of Abcoude to the city magistrates is more of a complaint than a request. Note that organ music is an offense likened to the wallpaper of a bordello. The request ends with an ironic—if not hilarious—flourish: the prohibition of organ music will be announced by the ringing of the bells.

Maarten Albert Vente. ***Bouwstoffen tot de geschiedenis van het nederlandse orgel in de 16e eeuw.*** **Amsterdam: H. J. Paris, 1942, 13–14 from Utrecht: National Archives, Archives of the Legislature of Utrecht, nr. 349, Register of Acts and Commissions 25, folio 313–14:**

ABCOUDE
    Request by the Reformed Consistory of Abcoude to the Legislature of Utrecht regarding the misuse of the organ.

    1649, December 7

    To the Right Honorable Lords Legislators of the Region of Utrecht, or their Right Honorable regular deputies

2 | PEOPLE

We the members of the consistory at Abcoude humbly declare that from a very long time ago it has been customary among the papists that in the church every year during the Christmas and New Year's season the organ is played every evening, and this has been continued to be done with us Reformed people because the court and church trustees, being mostly Pope-followers, have not wanted to prevent this, and in that way have given the common people such open doors to insolence, that they have not refrained from placing in the church such unsuitable decorations, making improper paintings on the walls and elsewhere, such that they should not even be tolerated in bordellos, and have even gone so far that they have covered the pulpit and other seats with filth, and that we the supplicants last year complained to the marshal of Abcoude, and that because of a prohibition by the aforesaid marshal the sexton has stopped the playing, but now we petitioners have experienced that members of the court, who are mostly Catholic, contrary to the aforementioned prohibition, have ordered the sexton to play for two hours every night during the upcoming Christmas and New Year's season, and such, for the reasons quoted earlier, should not be allowed and no new superstitions should be introduced into our holy reformation, so that the weeds that are being sown this way will not grow and the kingdom of the Antichrist be increased. Therefore, we the supplicants turn to you the honorable dignitaries to humbly request that you honorable lords will instruct the sexton and all others not to open the church during the evening in the coming Christmas and New Year's days, nor to play on the organ nor other [instruments] on penalties of a thousand double riders for each contravention above [in addition to] arbitrary correction. And that this judgment will be proclaimed in Abcoude with the ringing of the bells. Yours truly

[It was recorded in the margin:]

The deputies detest the insolence, the uncomely willfulness and profaning of the Christian and Reformed Church of God, as related above, deeming this not only intolerable, but also punishable according to the declarations and ordinances of the country and of the honorable members of the legislature, as others on behalf of the upper rulers of this district and lands of Utrecht, have previously published several times and confirmed concerning additional prohibitions and banns in this regard, which have been proclaimed at the appropriate places and times, (therefore we) explicitly order, decree, command, and forbid with these presents in the first place the sexton of the aforementioned church in Abcoude, and all others, to whom this might apply, not to open this church neither on coming Christmas or New Year's Day nor in the evening, nor to play the organ or other [instruments] inside, and even less to commit the aforesaid or other willfulness, insolence, or profaning on penalty of fifty gold double Dutch riders [dubloons] for each breaking or contravention of this ruling to be forfeited above arbitrated correction, etc. Made at Utrecht, the seventh of December 1649.

CONVENTIKEL OF THE HAGUE

Petition to the Church Council of The Hague (1642)

Sometimes the rhetoric in the pipe organ debate devolved into complete mockery, as shown by this petition that the members of the assembly (conventikel) submitted to the consistory of The Hague on January 3, 1642. Two entrenched camps of the organ controversy worshiped together (or attempted to) in The Hague. This petition mocks writings of the anti-orgelists—*a more illiterate, working class of worshipers. The deliberate run-on sentences, misspellings, jeering, and gossipy asides are intended as farcical parody.*

Koninklijke Bibliotheek, The Hague: Hs KA XLVIII, folio 630–33:

Petition to the Church Council of The Hague 1642

To the honorable gentlemen of the consistory, ministers, elders, and deacons of the Reformed church in The Hague

With all respect and proper reverence we submit, a large part of this same Reformed Christian church, as we petitioners have learned from reliable sources, that some outstanding brothers and sisters of this church have forgotten it because of an exceptionally large self-conceit, and hold separate meetings and assemblies at several places here, such as at the corner of the Wagenbrugge, on the corner of the Bagijnestraet, in the Achterom, in Veenstraet near the furriers, in the stock exchange at the market, in the

Eendeken, where these brothers and sisters go to examine closely,[1] pull their hair and cut into pieces in the sharpest possible manner, all of the sermons that had been preached the entire week, asking about their opinion of it, whether or not anything could be said about it, and whether this or that minister has not exceeded his bounds and would be punishable about it, as well as many other deep questions, which their dull and unsharpened brains could not fathom, such as when a husband rashly struck his wife in the mouth with his fist, whether she should simply bear it without objection, and accept that for now as a temporary weakness, and if the woman [wife] cannot understand this, and she then struck him in the nose with her fist so that his nose is half flattened, he Sir Henrick Laermans, should not also take this as a weakness in his wife, which happened once between them, and which led to a major quarrel, at these meetings the matter of the organ was discussed, the petitions created, the booklet by the Earl of Suijlicum[2] examined point by point, debated and condemned, considered as wicked, these and other things which have been permitted by many honorable, God-fearing, and wise men at the national synod at Dordrecht and considered as unimportant, because salvation does not depend on it. However, these zealous and strained pure brothers and sisters have received the Holy Spirit in a greater measure as they mean they are endowed with much more wisdom than all those God-fearing men, they find such great concern in this, and they are so affected that some of the aforementioned brothers, when the organ played for the first time during the Psalms, [they] were so overcome that they became feverish and had to go home and have a drink and had to lie down to rest, which made all the others also fear that they would get the fever, which thus makes these people rant and rave as if they were crazy, but if we petitioners had intended to object to this with requests and complaints, our group would be so large, that these seditious, riotous, and disquieted people are so weak, knowing that this matter does not really touch our salvation, and trusting you honorable gentlemen completely, have therefore not wanted to bother your honors with such trivial matters, which these disquieted and conceited brothers and sisters (enemies of the music and the organ) your honors trusting but with an even better order intend to put, these people become daily more and more odious among the peaceful good and quiet congregation, which would have loved to see, that the order that is in use in most other towns and cities, to quiet all foul and

---

1. *eplucheren*, pick carefully; literally, to *husk*.
2. The Earl of Zuilichem, Constantijn Huygens.

2 | PEOPLE

false voices and keep them in check, also had wanted to continue, these people want to make this look popish-minded and hold it to be superstition, but they do not know that wisdom is kept under their caps, in the center of their forehead where the fools are cut by stone cutters, where the worm lives that makes them jerk without reason, they fight against their own shadow, they run but are not being chased, they yell and scream as if the dance master from Haarlem[3] is after them, they are ashamed to put their names under their petition, for the reason that there is not one notable person among them, but let us see what kind of folks these are, that maintain these foundations of division, we shall begin with the oldest and grayest beards, and those who should be the wisest, such as Mr. Calckman, the Earl Stockbeurs, Mr.[4] Laersemaker with his neighbor Rembeslager and furrier Joncker linen merchant in the crest of Spain, page Cnoopmake in the Achterom, alias Caelbeck in the Cortsteegh, Mr. Cleermaecker in the Achterom, the page Colhuijcken wool fuller, page Cooperslager, my gentleman Laerman, alias Cooman the Nose,[5] and the one that should be mentioned principally, doctor Simonen Lijsken that is able to write out all the sermons in his own way,[6] which he has also taught to some women, which are servant girls, and are called *geusecloppen*,[7] which sermons are sharply broken apart and beaten at these corrupt and hypocritical meetings. For this purpose, especially talented are doctor Simonen Lijsken and Mrs. Simonen Lijsken, his wife, who both were extravagant in this sham of holiness, and Miss Marie and others who participate when their masters and mistresses have gone outside The Hague, and which then make the cellars and bottle storage areas so pure, that when the masters come home again, and sometimes bring some friends or invite them, thinking that they had supplies in storage, they find the sheep shorn, the cellar pumped dry, the butter in the barrels melted away, the flour in the pan over the fire with some butter and eggs all dried up, the house neatly kept while their people are absent with four—five—six or more guests until eleven or twelve or one

3. *dansmeester van Haerlem* could be a euphemism for the devil.

4. *Monsr*, likewise the title for Mr. Cleermaecker.

5. The list of surnames certainly does not indicate members of The Hague elite! Respectively: Mr. Shoemaker, Mr. Button Maker, Mr. Bare Faced, Mr. Clothes Maker, and Mr. Tinker (maker of pots and pans), and Cooman "the Nose"!

6. In Amsterdam the sermon was frequently transcribed as well, often without the cooperation or approval of the minister, "so that he unexpectedly saw the product of his mind displayed for sale in the bookstores." Evenhuis, *Ook dat was Amsterdam*, 36.

7. A sixteenth-century designation for unmarried, pietistic women.

o'clock at night and even if its people are home, they arrive home at whatever hour and say that they have been for dinner at one friend or another, this happens now to the one and then to the other, and has happened frequently in the Raemstraat, who have noticed that, and among them there is also a brother from Voorburgh who for the sake of his good name is not named here,[8] and others could well learn from such restraint, this people has been given a great conscience and the spirit of candidness, this is the rabble that when a minister ascends the pulpit that they do not like [to] walk out of the church, even if they were seated in the middle of the people they stand up anyway as if they are unwell, and go to another church; these are the disturbers that are not ashamed to boast that they gather the most votes to elect the elders and deacons, who are thus elected, those votes that they have beforehand considered among each other and decided what they could accomplish in any way, whether by notes or otherwise, this froth of unreliability, they get together in the church office not to help elect sincere advocates for the poor, but to choose by their efforts absolutely (if they can bring it about) only those of whom they approve, just like Your Honors must have noticed at the last election of elders and deacons, forcefully opposing the election as elder of Mr. councilor Kinschot, only because they were afraid (if they had given one in reply) that he being a good man would be easily swayed to permit the organ, which they state they do not wish to happen, as being godless, etc., and even though they have been told that they are doing wrong to oppose the mentioned councilor for reasons, yet one of the smartest among them has defended this matter, as he was the best orator with a bare chin, even though his gray beard could have been present, who with considered counsel has researched the one and studied in his exchange office, the other in his candle melting pan, another one in his copper kettles, and yet another one in his hardware store, and another one yet that it is the most important that both men and women, who have been well educated, in their masters' and mistresses' cellar, and that confirmed with a double *roomer*, and then fastened with a large button, at Page Button Master properly buttoned down.[9]

To come to a conclusion and a request by the petitioners, it is not our intention to break Your Honors' head with many requests for the silencing of the organ, if Your Honors would so order, but we ask very reverently that

---

8. This could also be an indication that the "brother from Voorburgh" was a minister.

9. A play on the previously mentioned names, a reminder of their blue-collar, unschooled vocations.

2 | PEOPLE

you Honorable Gentlemen pay attention to these dangerous and seditious private meetings and conspiracies, not to take them lightly, and if this and similar assemblies[10] have been the beginning of many schisms, factions, sects, heresies and mutinies, such as the Hoeken and Cabeljauwen,[11] the *Knipperdollingsche* Mennonites,[12] Anabaptist re-baptizers, remonstrants and contra-remonstrants, and more recently the Taurentians[13] and these would become puritans, we the undersigned petitioners know that this cannot be stopped by Your Honors only, but trust that Your Honors could bring about consideration by the Court of Justice, or by the parliament, whatever Your Honors consider the most advisable, concerning the pamphlet inserted in the collection bag of the deacons instead of money, that is certainly strange, but a church would desire, or conquer a church, here attention needs to be paid as well, as to where this came from, it in noticeable that the popish-minded which can still have a church in every house, with each its own ornaments, its popes and monks, which daily swarm over the streets like bees and *clopsusters*[14] without number, that to this day take place throughout the land, in direct contravention of all decrees, that are only useful to line the pockets of the sheriffs and bailiffs, who leave them alone if they contribute, just like the sweet women[15] who are their decoys, that put many honest men in trouble, this encourages their lives and dominate, as sincere children, all this should be considered, for if you allow this fire to smolder this long, at last the flames will erupt, just like can be seen in England, Scotland, and Ireland on a daily basis, and we do not know how it will end, it could be hatched in this way, may God prevent it, therefore we petitioners highly recommend this matter to you Honorable Gentlemen to observe and in the most careful and the most appropriate way to provide in this matter, as you Honorable Gentlemen think appropriate.

10. *conventiculen*.
11. Two Dutch factions that fought each other in a civil war.
12. = Bernhard Knipperdolling (1495–1536) was a leader of the Münster Anabaptists.
13. Taurentians were warriors who were personal guards of administrators and high initiates.
14. Roman Catholic lay sisters.
15. *geriefelijcke vrouckens*, most likely a euphemism for "prostitutes."

3
Pastors

ANDREAS OSIANDER

Commentary on Psalm 150 (excerpt, 1524)

It was not only the Dutch Reformed who differed on the opinion of organ use. Here Lutheran minister Andreas Osiander (1498–1552) raises some interesting objections in 1524.

Andreas Osiander D. Ä. Gesmatausgabe, ed. Gerhard Müller. Vol. 2. Gütersloh: Gerd Mohn, 1975, 279:

They say, however, *It says in the Psalms, "Praise God with the strings and organ."* I reply, it is also written, *sun and moon, lightning, thunder, hail, snow, ice and wind should praise Him.* Thus I conclude that thunder and lightning should be played in the church, and that we should remove the roof so that snow and rain can fall in. But if God can be praised with thunder and lightning in such a way that they do not enter the church, then He can also be praised by the organ without that in the church as well. How can God be praised in thunder and lightning? When one recognizes his power and wisdom through them! Likewise one praises God with the organ when one recognizes his grace in giving humans such an art. But what does that have to do with the churches? A cobbler can and should praise God with his handiwork just as much as the organist, but he shouldn't make shoes in church. Thus, playing the organ is not contrary to the faith but contrary to love, because it irritates with its worldly songs and is otherwise useless and brings nothing, since it cannot speak nor instruct the listeners. Therefore, one should simply omit it.

HERMANNUM FAUKEEL

Marriage song sung to the glory of Jesus Christ (1628)

Hermannus Faukelius (1560–1625), minister of Middelburg, gives an early opinion on the use of the pipe organ in Reformed worship. Born in Brugge, Faukelius studied in Gent and Leiden and first ministered at the Church Under the Cross in Cologne from 1585 to 1599. Then he became minister in Middelburg from 1599 to 1625.[16] He wrote Kort begrip der Christelijke Religie, *a short catechism for local use, and was a delegate to the National Synod of Dordrecht (1618–1619). The sermon excerpt here concludes with a reluctant admission that the organ could be used in worship; but not before a warning about Catholic abuse of music, and that organ music can elicit all kinds of unchaste desires.*

---

16. Lieburg, "Participants At the synod of Dordt," 1:95.

Hermannum Faukeel, *Bruylofts-liet, ter eeren Jesu Christi gesonghen; inden 45. psalm, onder 't voorbeelt vanden coninck Juda, ende zijne bruyt: affbeeldende Christi gheestelijck houwelijck, met zijne heylighe kercke: Inhoudende de liefde, uyt welcke Christud zijne h. bruyt hem vertrouwt, ende de bruyt van hare.* **Middelburg: Symon Moulert, 1628, 18–21:**

Marriage song sung to the glory of Jesus Christ

And as the musical instruments, because of their lovely sound, have a special power to stir the people, therefore the Lord has also ordained musical instruments among the ceremonies of the law, to stir the Jewish people to sing the praise of the Lord and to joyfully proclaim his wondrous deeds. . . . therefore the people of the Old Testament were truly urged in Psalm 150: *Praise the Lord with the trumpets, the psalteries and the harps, praise him with tambourines and dancing, with strings and pipes, and with the clanging cymbals,* because God had ordained such playing of instruments in that age in the ceremonial worship service, but now in the New Testament it would be great foolishness to prescribe them for the people of God as a part of the external worship service: and in this way we correctly criticize the papists that retain the sound of the organs in their sanctuaries, as well as chimes and bells and cymbals as a part of the worship service by which God is honored and served; in the same way that they have taken many ceremonies for the Mass from the ceremonies of the Old Testament, and in that way want to defend this: and they are also of the opinion that they should serve God in this way even now, with the sound of the organ and of the trumpets, for it is written there *Praise the Lord with the sound of the organ and of strings*; as if the curtain of the temple had not been torn in two at the death of Christ, and in that way the ceremonies of the Old Testament not had been discontinued.

Truly this is more than heathen ceremonies and superstitions; nobody will be able to say against this that it appears to have been done improperly by us, that we appear to be the enemies of all instruments and strings because we criticize the Catholics for that. On the other hand, someone might say that the organs are now used in many Reformed churches and have been restored in them by some, even though they had been banned earlier.

3 | PASTORS

To this last thought we reply firstly that it has never been demanded of the churches or of the church-servants to erect or use them, yes when the synods were asked about this they replied that for many reasons it would be of more use to ban them than to construct them in the sanctuaries. But as the government in its authority has yet decreed this, we suffer this as an unimportant matter, even though it would be better if they were placed somewhere else rather than in the church where we serve the Lord; and just like Paul chastised the Corinthians because they held their common meals in the same place as they held their congregational meetings, saying *Do you not have houses to eat and to drink? Or do you despise the congregation of the Lord, and shame those who do not have anything?*[17] And furthermore, are there no other houses or spots to place such instruments for the entertainment of the people, so that you must use the churches for that?

Secondly, such playing of the organ should not be used as if God is served or honored by it, or to assign any worship of God in it: or to put it another way, we would revert to the ceremonies of the Old Testament, and at the same time descend into the superstitions of the people; therefore then let them be for the entertainment of the people, to draw the people into the church through such an occasion, and thus into the hearing of God's word, or to pull the people from the taverns etc. and to keep them there, that as long as they hear that, they at least do no evil, which are the reasons that are given for it, and I leave them to speak for themselves, they may count as ample as they want for unimportant things, but when they are to be used for the worship of God, and put religion in that, then they are no longer unimportant instruments, but superstition that would be better rejected rather than suffered.

As far as the playing of instruments in the houses, even though this is not mentioned at this time, thus I will only say in passing: that this is not evil in itself, but is good and permitted for the entertainment of people, just like David played for Saul when he was melancholy or depressed (1 Samuel 16:24) and Elisha also had someone play for him on an instrument when he was disturbed in his spirit (2 Kings 3:15) in order to be able to answer the kings Jehoshaphat and Joram with a quieter and more perfect feeling when they asked questions, but that they now abuse in frivolity and for dancing, and in order to further incite the hearts of the people to all types of lasciviousness and unchasteness, so that they spend all night doing this at weddings and dinners. We condemn that; for no one is edified by that but rather

17. 1 Corinthians 11:22.

many are tempted and it is a harmful abuse of the good gifts of God, i.e. music. And if it were to happen in this way it were to be desired that following the example of Christ the pipers and flute players and other musicians were chased from the house, rather than that the youth would be ruined by that, although most of the fault lies with the older folk who are not satisfied with simple and entertaining music at their table, but want that the musicians also serve the unrestrained youth, by playing all types of frilly dances, etc., and thus to further incite the unchaste desires, and draw the pious into sin, and the slandering of the holy Scriptures through such offenses. Let our entertainment be in the Lord in modesty and moderation and that the use of the musical instruments not lead us to immoderation to thus waste our time and thus neglect our calling; but that our spirit be uplifted though the moderate use of them, and be all the more alert and prepared to each carry out our calling. And this be enough said for the explanation of the decree of the Psalms and the proper understanding of them.

CHRISTOPH FRICK

Prayer of Dedication for the new Organ in Bardowick (1631)

Christoph Frick (1577–1640) was the son of Lutheran minister, Kaspar Frick, and received his education in Wittenberg. In 1605 Christopher returned to his hometown to support his father. But in 1618 he became the pastor at Bardowick, where he heroically saved the church building from iconoclastic threats. The prayer of dedication for the new organ in Bardowick, translated here in part, is personal and moving. Of note is Frick's concern for proper organ use: it must not itself be worshiped (as "the papists" are wont to do), nor should it be hated and torn down (as the Calvinists are wont to do)! Clearly, the middle way is that the organ be used properly for leading the worshiper's praise.

Dedicatory prayer for the new organ at Bardowick from Christophorum M. Friccium. *Music-Büchleins: oder Nützlicher Bericht von dem Uhrsprunge, gebrauche u. Erhaltung christl. Music u. also von d. Lobe Gottes . . . / durch Christophorum Friccium.*[1] **Luneburg: J. & H. Sternen, 1631, 333–34:**

O faithful, compassionate God. . . .

1. *Little Music Book, or Useful Report concerning the Origin, Use, and Preservation of Christian Music and thus Concerning the Praise of God, which Christians should carry out in the lower Choir of this miserable, afflicted vale of tears and woe. Which, however, they will carry out in part (after the songs of lament down here are sung and finished), there in the high bright-shining angel choir of the heavenly hall of peace and joy in unspeakable*

You have granted us your mercy and aid during these very trying times in the rebuilding of a new organ....

Yes, Lord, we would always be praising You. Your praise shall always be in our mouths and in our hearts. And, as this new organ has been built for Your praise and honor, so we want to offer up the same again to You in all humility. And [as this new organ] has been dedicated and set aside in this, Your house, to be a holy instrument and tool, [so we would be] asking you from the bottom of our hearts that You would accept and receive in all mercy the work that was begun and completed out of Christian reverence, and [that You would] by your divine presence sanctify and make holy the same.

Mercifully grant that it may never again either be misused by papists for superstition and idolatry, nor be torn down by Calvinists, nor, as happened before, be destroyed by tumults of war, nor be desecrated by any other means or methods. Rather, grant in Your fatherly way that it shall be used for Christian melodies, that Your name will thereby be honored, and [that its] listeners be quickened to Christian worship, be encouraged to listen attentively to Your Word, and be reminded of and prompted to gratitude for all Your spiritual and physical blessings.

---

delight and glory.

CHRISTOPHILUS EUBULUS

The Matters Necessary for Reformation (1678)

The Rev. Jacobus Koelman was an active second-generation Reformer, himself a student of Voetius. In both word and deed he lived out his convictions; when the plague visited his parish in 1666, he and his wife, Anna Huss, faithfully ministered to the sick regardless of their own safety. Here, Koelman writes defeatingly about organ use. It's clear that by 1677 synods were tired of the bickering, and the church had (mostly) now accepted organ music in the churches.

Theophilus Parresius[1] [= Jacobus Koelman], *Historisch verhael van de proceduuren tegen D. Jacobus Koelman, predicant tot Sluys in Vlaenderen, wegens zijn debvoiren tot reformatie ontrent het stuck der formulieren en feestdagen ; beschreven door Theophilus Parresius.* **Rotterdam: Pieter Hendricksz, 1677, 16:**

Historical account of the Procedures against Rev. Jacobus Koelman, Minister at Sluys in Flanders, because of his [attempts] at Reformations regarding the document about the Forms and Holy Days. Rotterdam 1677.

13 November 1672: Historical account:

---

1. In addition to *Theophilus Parresius*, Koelman also used the pseudonym *Christophilus Eubulus*.

We request in unity and sincerity, that you Honorables will ban from the service of God in our area the use of the organ, as it [the pipe organ] is a false novelty,[2] unknown to the Apostolic and old church, giving the sense of Jewishness, Heathenism, and Papistry. It does not serve to further and encourage spiritual involvement [or worshipers], but rather it prevents and diminishes that. And as our Synods state, they [the organs] make us forget the proper occasion and instead cause more ceremonies and musical instruments in the church. Because of this, worshippers fall into other superstitions, and so [the organs] were rejected in the first reformation in all Swiss, French, Scottish, Hungarian, German, and Dutch churches, as is obvious in the latter as shown fully by two of our national Synods, held in Dordrecht, in the years 1574 and 1578, art. 50 and art. 77.

Christophilus Eubulus [= Jacobus Koelman], *De pointen van nodige reformatie, omtrent de kerk, en kerkelijke, en belijders der gereformeerde kerke van Nederlandt.* Vlissingen: Abraham van Laaren, 1678, 186–7:

The matters necessary for reformation, regarding the church, the ecclesiastical, and members of the Reformed Church of the Netherlands:

In the twelfth place, regarding the singing, both publicly and privately in the homes, the following things are mentioned for improvement. In several large cities it is tolerated without objections by the ministers (yes, some even are starting to endorse it!) that the organ is used at, or around/before/during/and after the worship service to entertain the ears. Even though this is quite objectionable to others, before the singing begins the organ plays for quite awhile, and then the organ also plays during the singing, although that is not done in all places. After the singing is finished and the blessing has been pronounced, the organist resumes his playing and plays the tune of a psalm or hymn, or of a ditty, for the entertainment of those present or who stay in the church a while. It appears they are copying this from the Jewish tradition, from the heathens, or from the papistry; however, it was unknown to the Apostolic and old churches and it does not serve the enhancement and awakening of the Spirit, as some are wont to say, but rather to hinder and weaken them and, as the synods state, *to make people*

---

2. *quade nieuwigheidt.*

3 | PASTORS

forget the good which the synods have rejected, particularly those of the years 1574 and 1578 held at Dordrecht Art. 50 and 77, just like was done by the Swiss, French, Scottish, Hungarian, and German. But now no more effort is made against this by the synods of the Netherlands: the evil is now established and they [the synods] don't want to touch it.

ABRAHAM VAN DE VELDE

The Wonders of the Most High (excerpt, 1733)

Like Koelman before him, the Rev. Abraham van de Velde shows that time and synodical resolutions alone did not change everyone's attitudes towards the pipe organ in worship. Van de Velde doesn't offer new reasoning, but his work is interesting because it is so late: 1733. It is also clear that by this time hymnody, in addition to Psalmody, had found its way into the worship services of the Reformed.

The Wonders of the Most High or Indication of the causes, ways and means whereby the United Provinces, against the expectation of the whole world, were elevated in such a marvelous way from their previous oppression to such great power, riches, awe, and acclaim. As related by several eminent historians, and which after the manner of the time are compiled to a necessary and profitable use, by Abraham van de Velde. During his life, minister of the divine word of the Congregation of Jesus Christ at Middelberg. Amsterdam, by Pieter Visser, 1733. 410–11:

With one word, we judge this [organ use] and other novelties in these forgettable days a useless hindrance. This we also say of the introduction of new forms of songs and human hymns and present-day ditties, which we do not find in God's word, as also the playing and peeping of organs in the Church which things are all against the resolutions and decisions of the synods of our Fatherland. About singing in the church, see the National Synod held in Dordt in 1578, article 76; the National Synod held in Middelburg in 1581, article 51; the National Synod held in the Hague in 1586, article 62; where hymns not found in Scripture are expressly forbidden. It is known from church history that those who are after novelties by introducing man-made hymns and errors have corrupted the congregation, so warned Arius, Samosatenus, and Valentians in Nichephor volume 9, chapter 24; Eusebius in volume 7, chapter 24; and Tertullian in *Carne Christi*, chapters 17 and 20 of volume 2. Although these people, who have proposed these new things, have no wrong motives, it is nevertheless not advisable to follow in their steps at this time, since we may perceive copper as gold, as the learned Peter Martyr witnesses about the [time] hymns [were] introduced into the Roman Catholic Church. See him [Peter Martyr] on I Corinthians 14:26. The words of Lord van Aldegonde in this respect are remarkable. In the introduction to his book of Psalms [he writes], *The experience of earlier days in God's worship has taught us indeed that it is often harmful to introduce something which is not grounded on the Scriptures of the Old and New Testaments.*

About the discontinuation of, and regulations for, the organs can be seen the resolutions of the Synods of Dordt, 1578, article 77; of Middelburg, 1581; also those of Gelderland, 1640, article 3, which have all dealt with ter-minating the organ when determining the place of the organ in the church. Special attention should be paid to what was already stated and decided by the Synod of Dordt held in the year 1574 in this matter. There we read *concerning the use of the organ in the congregation, we hold that according to 1 Corinthians 14:10, it* [the organ] *should not have a place in the church; and where it is still used when people leave the church, it is of no use but to forget what was heard before.* They testify that it [organ music] is nothing but frivolity. It is also remarkable that the Lord Rivet, contending against the papists, mentions several of their authors who condemn the novelty of the organ, and points out that it [the organ] is without profit. See Rivet in *Catholic Orthodoxy*, volume 1, page 561. If one wishes to know the reasons why organs should be kept out of the church, read our learned theologians in their disputations against Lutherans and Papists. See Faukeel, about Psalm 45, page 20. Also Larenus, in Chapter 12 of Esa, page 47, where we find the story of the duty of Middelburg's consistory to do away with the organ. [Johannes] Hoornbeek disputation 2, *De Psalmodia*, Thesis 7; Rivet, in *Exodus* Chapter 15 verse 12; the work of Gisbertus Voetii in *Politica Ecclesiastica*, Volume 1, page 548; Hospinianus in *De Templis*, page 309. Humanly speaking, it would be better if this and other novelties were not mentioned.

ÆGIDIUS FRANCKEN

Conclusion of sermon on Psalm 150:3–4 (1734)

In contrast to Revs. van de Velde's and Koelman's admonitions, one year later and but sixty-four miles away, the Rev. Francken accepted the gift of a new organ for his church in Maassluis. Not only that, but he preached a sermon extolling the virtues of the pipe organ, and from the pulpit publicly thanked the donor, Mr. van Wyn.

Ægidius Francken: *Heilig gebruik des orgels, vertoont in een leer-reden over Psalm CL. vers III–VI. Gedaan op de inwyding van't Maassluische orgel. Met een toegift van een leer-reden over het verborgen manna en de witte keursteen.* Delft: Pieter van der Kloot, 1734. 106ff:

. . . . But before I conclude my sermon, I cannot fail to render the duty which I owe to you Honorable Councilors. Honorable and esteemed Mr. Govert van Wyn, who has so carried out so lustrously the duties of being treasurer of the fisheries for twenty-six years, and with your wise judgement and close attention has contributed so many thousands to benefit the fisheries of Maassluis. It is not my intent here to enumerate and to glorify your special charity, which you have bestowed on so many needy people, or to publicly bring our thanksgiving for the very great evidence of the favors with which you have, with undeserved generosity, not only bestowed our deacons over several years by donating to them a hundred and four mourning cloaks[1] so that they could be rented out for the support of our needy; yes, even this year you have decorated this town with a convenient brick staircase with an iron railing for whose masonry you have borne most of the cost. But today particularly we are persuaded to express our due gratitude for the costly showpiece of this organ which you have donated to the church of Maassluis out of sheer generosity and unsolicited, and as well in a free show of generosity have funded a worthy yearly salary for the organist.

Therefore, highly esteemed honorable gentleman, I, on behalf of all the residents of Maassluis, want to express my sincere thanks for this unequaled present of this beautiful instrument for the furtherance of the Lord God, the abundant spring of all true blessing. May God reward you, sir, abundantly for this unprecedented showing of love, and not omit your labor of love done for His house.

Yes, may the Almighty be your abundant gold and mighty silver. The merciful God, who has kindled your heart in compassion to come to the aid of the suffering and to make the hearts of the widows sing with joy, will cause the poor will bless you when they are warmed by the skins of your lambs.[2] May The Ancient of Days, in whose hands rest our years, and who has granted that on this day you may reach the exceptional age of ninety years, grant you, esteemed sir, long and prosperous health. [May He] keep and renew the fortunes not only of your soul, but also the abilities of your body like those of an eagle. May He crown your gray hairs with His favor and with that true crown which is found in the way of justice.

To this our heart says, *Amen*. May the Lord accomplish this, and confirm the heartfelt desire proclaimed this hour by Your servant, and all the people will say AMEN.

---

1. *Rouw-mantels.*
2. Another reference to van Wyn's gift of 104 rouw-mantels for the town's poor.

BIBLIOGRAPHY

Aa, van der, Abraham Jacob, et al. *Biographisch Woordenboek der Nederlanden.* 21 vols., 1852–1878. Haarlem: J. J. van Brederode.

Aimonus, floriacensis. *Historiae Francorum libri quinque.* Paris: Wechelem, 1567.

Alliance petition of 3 January 1642. Koninklijke Bibliotheek, The Hague. Hs. KA XLVIII, folio 632 and 633.

Alting, Heinrich. *Exegesis logica et theologica Augustane Confessionis, cum appendice problematica: num Ecclesiae Reformatae in Germania pro sociis Augustanae Confessionis agnoscendae et habendae sing: accessit syllabus controversiarum quae Reformatis hodie intercedunt cum Lutheranis.* Amsterdam: Jansen, 1647.

Amalarii Epsicopi Opera Liturgica Omnia, edited by John Michael Hanssens. Citta del Vaticano: Biblioteca Apostlica Vaticana, 1948.

Ames, William. *A Fresh Suit Against Human Ceremonies in God's Worship.* Amsterdam: G. Thorp, 1633.

Andreas Osiander D. Ä. Gesmatausgabe. Vol. 2, edited by Gerhard Müller. Gütersloh: Gerd Mohn, 1975.

Anglicus, Bartholomaeus. *De proprietatibus rerum.* Nuremberg: A. Koberger, June 20, 1492.

Annales Regni Francorum inde ab a. 741. usque ad a. 829, edited by Friedrich Kurze and Georg Heinrich. Pertz. Hannoverae : Hahniani, 1895.

Augustine, Aurelius. *Ennarrationes in Psalms 101–150,* edited by Franco Gori. Vol. 5. Vienna: Publishing house of the Austrian Academy of Sciences, 2005.

———. *Augustinus. Bekenntnisse und Gottesstaat. Sein Werk ausgewählt von Joseph Bernhart.* Frankfurt am Main: Insel-Verlag, 1987.

Aventinus, Johannes. *Joannis Aventini Annales ducum Boiariae.* Munich: Emperor, 1881.

Baile, Guillaume. *Controversiarum Catechismus,* edited by Henrico Lamormain. Vienna: Matthæus Formica, 1626.

Bale, John. *Acta romanorum Pontificum.* Basel: Oporinus, 1558.

Baronius, Caesar. *Annales Ecclesiastici.* Romae: s.n., 1588.

Basilius, Caesariensis. *Divi Basilii Magni Archiepiscopi Caesareae Cappadociae Omnia, Qvae Ad Nos Extant, Opera.* Basel: Froben, 1555.

Batelier, Jacob Johannes. *Examen accuratum disputationis primae & quasi inauguralis D. Gisberti Voetii, quam proposiut in Illustri Gymnasio Ultrajectino die 3. Sept. stylo vet. Anno 1634, ad pastores totius Provinciae & Quoscumque theologiae studiosos*. Utrecht: Van Someren, 1634.

Bellarmine, Roberto Francesco Romolo. *De Bonis Operibus in Particulari. Disputationes de controversiis Christianae fidei adversus huius temporis Haereticos*. Ingolstadt: Sartorius, 1586.

Bernard of Clairvaux. *Meditationes de interiori homine*. Basel: Johannes Amberbach, 1492.

———. *Liber de modo bene vivendi ad sororem* in *Patrologia Latina*, edited by Jacques-Paul Migne. Paris: D'Ambroise, 1859.

Bèza, Théodore de. *Acta colloquii Montis Belligartensis*. Turingae: Gruppenbach, 1587.

Bouchel, Laurent. *Decretorum Ecclesiae Gallicanae: ex conciliis eiusdem oecumenicis, statutis synodalibus, patriarchicis, prouincialibus, ac dioecesanis, regijs constitutionibus, senatusconsultis, episcoporum Galliae scriptis, alijsque cum veterum tum recentiorum monimentis collectorum libri VIII*. Paris: S. Cramoisy, 1621.

Brenz, Johannes. *De Poenitentia, Et Iis Quae Ad Poenitentiam Agendam necessaria sunt, Homili[a]e viginti quinq[ue]*. Halae Suevorum: Brubachius, 1544.

Brusch, Kaspar. *Monasteriorum Germaniae praecipuorum ac maxime illustrium: centuria prima*. Inglostadt: Alexandrum et Samuelem Vueyssenhornios fratres, 1551.

Bulengeri, Julii Caesaris. *De circo romano ludisque circensibus, ac circi et amphitheatrie venatione*. Paris: Robertum Nivelle, 1598.

———. *De theatro, ludiscuq scenicis libri duo*. Tricasses: Petri Cheuillot, 1603.

Cæremoniale episcoporum Clementis VIII. primum nunc denuo Innocentii Papae X auctoritate recognitum. Rome: Camerae Apostolicae, 1600.

Cajetan, Tommaso de Vio. *Summula Caietani: Reverendiss. Dn. Thomae de Vio Caietani Cardinalis S. Xysti, perquàm docta, resoluta ac compendiosa de peccatis Summula*. Paris: Claude Chevallon, 1530.

Calckman, Jan Jansz. *Antidotum, tegen-gift vant gebruyck of on-gebruyck vant orgel inde kercken der Vereenighde Nederlanden*. 's-Gravenhage: Aert van Meurs, 1641.

Calderwood, David. *The altar of Damascus or the patern of the English hierarchie, and Church policie obtruded upon the Church of Scotland*. Amsterdam: Giles Thorpe, 1621.

Carthusianus, Dionysius. *Vita sacerdotum*. Antwerp: Guilielmum Vorstermannum, 1517.

Clemens, Aurelius Prudentius. *Liber Apotheosis*. Oeniponti: Wagner, 1876.

Clementis Alexandrini . . . omnia quae quidem extant opera, edited by Gentian Hervet. Paris: Sonnius, 1572.

Colin, Marie-Alexis, ed. *French Renaissance Music and Beyond: Studies in Memory of Frank Dobbins*. Epitome Musical. Turnhout, Belgium: Brepols, 2019.

Constitutions and canons ecclesiastical . . . London: Robert Barker, printer to the Kings most excellent Maiestie, 1603.

Corpus iuris canonici 2: Decretalium collections, edited by Aemilius Ludwig Richter and Emil Friedberg. Leipzig: Bernhardi Tauchnitz, 1879.

Cudsemius, Petrus. *Tractatus Brevis, De Desperata Calvini Causa: Lectu non minus utilis, atque iucundus; In Quo Sectae Calvinisticae non tam picta effigies, quam vivum corpus, cuivis spectandum ad oculum exhibetur*. Coloniae: Gualterus, 1612.

Desmarets, Samuel. *Theologus paradoxus retectus et refutatus, sive Samuelis Maresii exercitationes aliquot academicae oppositae duodecim paradoxis, et plus aequo virulentis disuptationibus, ex professo contra ipsum habitis in lycaeo Ultrajectino, auctore et praeside d. Gisb. Voetio, ibidem primario theologo; cujus centum assertiones lubricate, periculosae et plane paradoxae, bona fide referuntur et confutantur*. Groningen: Joannis Nicolai, 1649.

Drusius, Johannes. *Annotationum in totum Jesu Christi testamentum sive praeteritorum libri decem.* Franekeræ: Aegidius Radaeus, 1612.
Duker, Arnoldus Cornelius. *Gisbertus Voetius.* Leiden: E. J. Brill, 1910.
Duranti, Ioannes Stephanus. *De ritibus ecclesiae catholicae.* Rome: Typography Vaticana, 1591.
Durantis, Guilelmus. *Rationale Divinorum officiorum.* Venice: Zalterius, 1599.
Dyer, Joseph. "The Place of *Musica* in Medieval Classifications of Knowledge." *The Journal of Musicology* 24:1 (2007) 3–71.
Eckhardus, Henricus. *Fasciculus Controversiarum Theologicarum. Quaestiones Fere Omnes Atque Singulas De Quibus Inter Augustanae Confessionis Theologos & Calvinianos disceptatur, continens: Et Praeter Adversariorum sententias propriis ipsorum verbis in quaestionibus singulis descriptas, eorundem argumenta ex Zvinglii, Oecolampadii, Calvini, Martyris, Musculi, Aretii, Danaei, Bezae, Ursini, Zanchii, Sohnii, Sadeelis, Iunii, Polani, Bucani, Piscatoris, Trelcarii, Keckermanni, Perkinsii, Nahumi [. . .] exhibens.* Lipsiae: Grosse, 1607.
Einhardus, Hilduin. *Annales Regum Francorum, Pipini, Caroli Magni & Lodovici.* Cologne: Birckmann, 1561.
Engle, Randall Dean. *Sound Theology: Pipe Organ Power Plays among the Protestants, Pulpits, Professors, and Peers.* Eugene, OR: Cascade, 2024.
———. "Voetius Outscored." In *Semper Refromanda: John Calvin, Worship and Reformed Traditions,* edited by Barbara Pitkin, 143–62. Göttingen: Vandenhoeck & Ruprecht, 2018.
Erasmus, Desiderius. *Desiderii Erasmi Roterodami Opera omnia.* Leiden: Van der Aa, 1703–1706.
———. *In novum Testamentum annotations.* Basel: Froben, 1540.
Erpino, Thomo. *Psalmi Davidis regis et prophetae, lingua syriaca.* Leiden: Lugduni Batavorum: Typographia Erpeniana, 1625.
Etymologicon magnum: seu verius lexicon saepissime vocabulorum origines indagans ex pluribus lexicis scholiastis et grammaticis anonymi cuiusdam opera concinnatum, edited by Thomas Gaisford. Oxonii: ex Typographo Academico, 1848.
Evenhuis, Rudolf Barteld. *Ook dat was Amsterdam: De kerk der hervorming in de Gouden Eeuw.* Amsterdam: Ten Have, 1967.
Faukeel, Hermannum. *Bruylofts-liet, ter eeren Jesu Christi gesonghen; inden 45. psalm, onder 't voorbeelt vanden coninck Juda, ende zijne bruyt: affbeeldende Christi gheestelijck houwelijck, met zijne heylighe kercke: Inhoudende de liefde, uyt welcke Christud zijne h. bruyt hem vertrouwt, ende de bruyt van hare.* Middelburg: Symon Moulert, 1628.
Filesac, Jean. *Ionnis Filesaci Selectorum liber secundus.* Paris: Mathurini Du Puis, 1631.
Felinus, Aretius [Martin Bucer]. *Psalmorum libri quinque ad Hebraicam veritatem traducti: et summa fide, parique diligentia à Martino Bucero enarrati. Eiusdem commentarii in librum Iudicum, & in Sophoniam Prophetam.* Geneva: Oliua Roberti Stephani, 1554.
Floriacensis, Aimonius Monachus. *Historiae Francorum libri quinque.* Vol. 4. Paris: Wechel, 1567.
Francken, Ægidius. *Heilig gebruik des orgels, vertoont in een leer-reden over Psalm CL. vers III–VI. Gedaan op de inwyding van't Maassluische orgel. Met een toegift van een leer-reden over het verborgen manna en de witte keursteen.* Delft: Pieter van der Kloot, 1734.
Friccium, Christophorum M. *Music-Büchleins: oder Nützlicher Bericht von dem Uhrsprunge, gebrauche u. Erhaltung christl. Music u. also von d. Lobe Gottes . . . / durch Christophorum Friccium.* Luneburg: Gedruckt bey J. & H. Sternen, 1631.

BIBLIOGRAPHY

Fumus, Bartholomaeus. *Summa aurea armilla nuncupata: casus omnes ad animarum curam attinentes, breviter complectens.* Venetiis: Franciscum Binodum, 1558.

Génébrard, Gilbert. *Gilb. Genebrardi theologi Parisiensis . . . Chronographiae libri quatuor. Priores duo sunt de rebus veteris populi, & præcipuis quatuor millium annorum gestis. Posterior, à D. Arnaldi Pontaci Vasatensis episcopi Chronographia aucti, recentes historias reliquorum annorum complectuntur. . . . Subiuncti sunt libri Hebræorum chronologici eodem interprete.* Paris: Martini Iuuenem via S. Ioan. Lateranensi, 1585.

Grotii, Hugonis. *Annotationes in Novum Testamentum.* Amsterdam: Ioh. & Cornelium Blaeu, 1641.

Gutherius, Jacobus. *De jure manium, seu de ritu, more et legibus prisci fineris libri 1.* Paris: Nicolaum Buon, 1615.

Heimenbergius, Ionnes. *De organis et canu organico in Sacro [sub præsidio Gisberti Voetii].* Ultraiecti: Ægidii Roman, 1641

Hieronymus, Sophronius Eusebius. *Sancti Eusebii Hieronymi Stridonensis Presbyteri, Commentariorum in Epistolam ad Ephesios libri tres*, edited by Jacques Paul Migne. Paris: J. P. Migne, 1845.

Huygens, Constantijn. *Gebruyck of ongebruyck van 't orgel in de kercken der Vereenighde Nederlanden.* Leiden: Bonaventuer ende Abraham Elsevier, 1641; Amsterdam: Arent Gerritsz. Vanden Heuvel, 16592, 16603.

——. *Use and Non-Use of the Organ in the Churches of the United Netherlands.* Translated by Erika E. Smit-van Rotte. New York: Institute of Mediaeval Music, 1964.

Irwin, Joyce, ed. *Anna Marie van Schurman: Whether a Christian Woman Should be Educated and Other Writings from Her Intellectual Circle.* Chicago: University of Chicago Press, 1998.

Joannou, Pericles-Pierre. *Discipline générale antique (IVe–IXe s.).* Grottaferrata: Pontificia Commissione per la Redazione del Codice di Diritto Canonico Orientale, 1962.

Josephus, Falvius. *Flavii Iosephi Antiqvitatvm Ivdaicarvm*, edited by Sigmund Gelen & Desiderius Eramsus. Basel: Froben, 1559.

Julianus, Falvius Claudius. *Juliani Imp[eratori] Opera, qvae qvidem potvervnt, omnia. Ea verò partim antehac edita, partim nunc primùm è manuscriptis eruta.* Paris: Cramoisy, 1633.

Kenyon, John Philipps, ed. *The Stuart Constitution 1603–1688: Documents and Commentary.* Cambridge: Cambridge University Press, 1969.

Krantz, Albrecht. *Metropolis sive historia ecclesiastica Saxoniae, Alberti Crantzii.* Coloniæ: Geruinum Calenium & hæredes Quentelios, 1574.

Lactantius, Lucius Coelius Firmianus. *L[ucii] Coelii Lactantii Firmiani Divinarum institutionum Libri VII.* Basel: Cratander, 1521.

Langhecrucius, Joannes. *De malorum horum temporum causis et remediis, deque Divinis officiis debite peragendis. Canonicorum et aliorum Ecclesiasticorum speculum.* Douai: Jean Bogard, 1584.

Lapide, Cornelius á. *Commentaria in sacram Scripturam*, Xysto Riario Sfortiae, edited by Neapoli: I. Nagar, 1854.

Lavertus, Ludwig. *In libros paralipomenon sive chronicorum Ludovici Lavateri Tigurini commentaries.* Zurich: Froschouerus, 1573.

Lieburg, Fred van. "The Participants At the synod of Dordt." In *Acta et Documenta Synodi Nationalis Dordrechtanae (1618–1619)*, edited by Donald Sinnema, Christian Moser, and Herman J. Selderhuis, 95. Göttingen: Vandenhoeck & Ruprecht, 2015.

Lindanus, Guilelmus Damasus. *Panoplia evangelica, sive De verbo Dei evangelico libri qvinqve: Quibus ex Scriptura Prophetica & Apostolica illius eruitur, & declaratur indoles atq[ue] natura. Partes explicantur, Scriptum atq[ue] [bagoaphor], Non scriptum, & quae ad Traditiones indubitatò Apostolicas, licèt non scriptas, at fide tamen pari suscipiendas pertinent, pertractantur. Denique verbum Dei non scriptum, sed traditum, adversus infesta Catholicae Christi Iesu Ecclesiae hostium tela, & arietationes omnes defenditur.* Cologne: Maternus Cholinus, 1560.

Lorinus, Johannes. *Commentarius in Sapientiam.* Lugduni: Horatij Cardon, 1601.

Mansi, Giovanni Domenico. *Sacrorum conciliorum nova et amplissima collectio, cujus Johannes Dominicus Mansi et post ipsius mortem Florentius et Venetianus editores ab anno 1758 ad annum 1798 priores triginta unum tomos ediderunt, nunc autem continuatat et absolut.* Vol. 32. Paris: H. Welter, 1901–1927 [v. 32, 1902].

Mantuanus, Baptista Spagnuoli. *F. Baptistae Mantvani carmelitae theologi, fastorvm libri dvodecim.* Strasbourg: Schurer, 1518.

Maxwell, John. *Episcopacie not abivred in His Maiesties realme of Scotland containing many remarkable passages newly pvblished, the contents of the severall chapters follow in the next page.* London: s.n., 1641.

Melanchthon, Philip. *Loci communes rerum theologicarum seu hypotyposes theologicae.* Wittenberg: Melchoir d. J. Lotter, 1521.

Meurius, Ioannis. *Glossarium, graeco-barbarum.* Lugduni Batavorum: Ludouicum Elzeuirium, 1614.

Micraelius, Johannes. *Syntagma historiarum Ecclesiae.* Stetini: Georgii Rhetii, 1644.

Molani, Johannes. *De canonici libri tres: I. De canoniorum vita. II. De eorum officijs. III. De dominio canonicorum & seruis ecclesiarum. Item, Orationes tres, De agnis Dei, De decimis dandis, De decimis defendendis cum trib. Indicibus.* Coloniae: Birckman, 1587.

Musculus, Wolfgang. *In ambas Apostoli Pauli ad Corinthios Epistolas Commentarii.* Basel: Ioannem Heruagium, 1559.

Navarrus [Martin Aspilcueta]. *Enchiridion sive manuale de oratione, et horis canonicis: ante annos quadraginta sermone Hispano Conymbricae compositum [et] aeditum . . . deinde Romae anno 1577 recognitum, auctum, [et] latinitate donatum . . . nunc autem denuo recognitum, emendatum, auctum, [et] se melius factum.* Rome: Tornerij & Berichiae, 1586.

Nebrissensis, Antonius. *In Quinquaginta Sacrae Scripturae Locos Non Vulgariter Enarratos Tertia Quinquagena.* Basileæ: n.p., 1543.

Nicene and Post-Nicene Fathers, First Series. Edited by Philip Schaff. Peabody, MA: Hendrickson, 1995.

Opera D. Gregorii Papae: Hvivs Nominis Primi, Cognomento Magni, Omnia Qvae Extant, Accvratissima Diligentia à mendis multis, vti lector facile . . . deprehendet, maximè in libris Epistolarum, repurgata . . . Cum Indice duplici, altero rerum, uerborum, sententiarumq[ue]: altero locorum S. scripturae explicatorum: utroq[ue] magna sedulitate conscript. Ulrich Koch, ed. Basiliae: Frobenius Et Episcopius, 1564.

Peraldus, Guillelmus. *Summae virtutum ac vitiorum.* Paris: Petrum Billaine, 1629.

Perkins, William. *Guil. Perkinsi Problema de Romanae fidei ementito Catholicismo.* Hanover: Antonium, 1611.

Pio, Alberto, de Carpi. *Ad Erasmi Roterodami expostulationem responsio accurata et paraenetica.* Fabio Forner, Biblioteca della Rivista di Storia et Letteratura Religiosa, testi e document, 17. Florence: Leo Olschki, 2002

BIBLIOGRAPHY

Piscator, Johannes. *In librum Psalmorum commentarius; Addita est in fine versio Psalmorum nova.* Herbornae: Corvinus, 1611.

Plantina, Bartholomaeus. *B. Platinae Cremonensis De Vita & moribus summorum Pontificum historia. Cui aliorum omniu[m], qui post Platinam uixerunt ad haec usque tempora, Pontificum res gestae sunt additae, nunquam antehac in uulgus datae.* Cologne: Hittorp, 1529.

Platina, Bartholomaeus. *B. Platinae Cremonensis De Vita & moribus summorum Pontificum historia. Cui aliorum omniu[m], qui post Platinam uixerunt ad haec usque tempora, Pontificum res gestae sunt additae, nunquam antehac in uulgus datae.* Cologne: Hittorp Cervicornus, 1529.

Pollux, Iulius. *Iulii Pollucis Onomasticon, hoc est, instructissimum rerum ac synonymorum dictionarium . . . cum praefatione sim. grynaei ad ludimagistros.* Basel: Robertum Winter, 1541.

Procopius of Gaza. *Commentarii in octateuchum, hoc est, in priores octo Veteris Testamenti libros.* Zurich: Gesner, 1555.

Resolutieboek Sneek, 1580–1663. Oud Archief Sneek Invoice Number 1: folio 42. Sneek: April 17, 1602.

Ressonaeo, Antonio Monchiaceno Demochare. *Missarum Celebratione* in *Christianae religionis institutionisque Domini nostri Jesu-Christi et apostolicae traditionis, adversus misoliturgorum blasphemias ac novorum hujus temporis sectariorum imposturas.* Paris: Frémy, 1562.

Rivet, André. *Commentarius in Psalmorum propheticorum de mysteriis evangelicis dodecadem selectam.* Lugduni Batavorum: I. & J. Commelini, 1626.

Sabellicus, Marcus Antonius Coccius. *Rapsodiae historiarum Enneadum Marci Antonii Coccii Sabellici. Continens sex Enneades reliquas cum earundem repertoriis & epitomis.* Paris: Parvus, 1528.

Sacrosancta Concilia Ad Regiam Editionem Exacta. 6: Ab anno DCXLIX. ad annum DCCLXXXVII, edited by Philippe Labbé. Venetiis: Coleti Et Albrizzi, 1729.

Salmasius, Claudius. *Claudii Salmasii Plinianæ Exercitationes in Caji Julii Solini Polyhistora.* Trajecti ad Rhenum: Johannem van de Water, Johannem Ribbium, Franciscum Halma, & Guilielmum van de Water, 1629.

Sanchez, Tomas. *Opus morale in praecepta Decalogi.* Lyon: Horatii Cardon, 1615.

Schoock, Martinus. *Exercitationes variæ, de diversis materiis, quae hac editione nova tum locupletatae et vindicatæ.* Trajecti ad Rhenum: Gisbertus à Zyll, 1663.

Schulting, Cornelius. *Bibliotheca Ecclesiastica catholica, sive refutatio totius theologiae Calvinianae.* Cologne: Stephanus Hemmerden, 1599.

———. *Hierarchica anacrisis, (seu), Animadversionvm et variarvm lectionvm libri sexdecim.* Cologne: Stephanus Henningius, 1604.

Schuberth, Dietrich. *Kaiserlice Liturgie: die Einziehung von Musikinstrumenten, insbesondere der Orgel, in den frühmittelalterlichen Gottesdienst.* Gottigen: Vandenoeck & Ruprecht, 1968.

Scoti, Mariani. *Chronica ad Euangelij ueritatem, post Hebraicae sacrosanctae scripturae & septuaginta interpretum uariationem, magno iudicio discussam & correctam, certa enumeratione temporum conscripta. Adiecimus Martini Poloni archiepiscopi Consentini, eiusdem argumenti Historiam.* Basel: Jacobus Parcus, 1559.

Stephano, Henrico. *Thesaurus Graecae linguae. Ab Henrico Stephano constructus.* Geneve: Galliarum Regis, 1572.

Suarez, Francisco. *Operis de Religione Tomus Secundus.* Lugduni: Iacobi Cardon, 1630.

Theiner, Augustino, ed. *Acta genuina SS. œcumenici Concilii Tridentini, nunc primum integra ed. ab A. Theiner*. Zagrabiae: Typis et sumptibus Societatis bibliophilae, 1874.

Tilenus, Daniel. *Syntagmatis tripertiti disputationum theologicarum in Academia Sedanensi habitarum, pars prima [-altera]*. Genevæ: Petrum & Jacobum Choue, 1622.

Turrianus, Francisco de. *Fratris Raphaelis de la Torre . . . De partibus potentialibus iustitiae in secundam secundae D. Thomae à quaestione LXXX vsque ad quaestionem CXXIII . . . Tomus primus, De religione et eius actibus*. Salmanticae: Franciscum de Cea Tesa, 1611.

Ussher, James. *Annales Veteris Testamenti, a prima mundi origine dedvcti: una cum rerum asiaticarum et ægyptiacarum chronico, a temporis historici principio usque ad Maccabaicorum initia product*. London: Crook & Baker, 1650.

Valencia, Gregorio de. *Gregorii de Valentia Metimnensis, Commentariorum theologicorum tomi 4. In quibus omnes quaestiones, quae continentur in Summa theologica D. Thomae Aquinatis, ordine explicantur ac suis etiam in locis controuersiae omnes fidei elucidantur Tomus primus quartus . . . Cum variis indicibus*. Lugduni: Horatij Cardon, 1619.

Vente, Maarten Albert, and Christiaan Cornelius Vlam, eds. *Documentaet archivalia ad historiam musicae neerlandicae. Bouwstenen voor een geschiedenis der toonkunst in de Nederlanden*. Utrecht: Vereniging voor Nederlands muziekgeschiedenis, 1965.

Vergile, Polydore. *De Rerum Inventoribus*. Venice: Christophorus de Pensis, 1499.

Viguier, Jean. *Instituiones ad Christianam Theologiam*. Venice: Rubinum, 1571.

Vitruvius, Marcus Pollio. *Marci Vitruvii Pollionis De architectura libri decem. Ope codicis Guelferbytani, editionis principis, ceterorumque subsidiorum recensuit, et glossario in quo vocabula artis propria Germ. Italian Gall. et Angl. explicantur, illustravit Augustus Rode*, edited by August Rode. Berlin: Mylius, 1800.

Voetius, Gisbertus. *Politicæ Ecclesiasticæ Partis Primae Libri Duo Priores*. Amsterdam: Joannis à Waesberge, 1663; *Politicæ Ecclesiasticæ Partis Primae Libri Duo Posteriores*. Amsterdam: Joannis à Waesberge, 1666; *Politicæ Ecclesiasticæ Pars Secunda*. Amsterdam: Joannis à Waesberge, 1669; *Politicæ Ecclesiasticæ Pars Tertia et Ultima*. Amsterdam: Joannis à Waesberge, 1676.

———. *Thersites Heautontimorumenos. Hoc est, Remonstrantium Hyperaspistes, Catechesi, et Liturgiae Germanicae, Gallicae & Belgicae Denuo Insultans, Retusus; Idemque Provocatus ad Probationem Mendaciorum, & Calumniarum Quae in Illustr[es] DD. Ordd. [Dominos Ordinatos] et ampl[issimos] Magistratus Belgii, Religionem Reformatam, Ecclesias, Synodos, Pastores, etc. sine ratione, sine modo effudit*. Utrecht: Abrahami ab Herwiick & Hermanni Ribbii, 1635

Whitgift, John. *An answere to a certen Libel intituled An admonition to the Parliament*. London: Henrie Bynneman for Humfrey Tay, 1572.

Zepper, Wilhelm. *Legum Mosaicarum forensium explanatio: Ubi quæstio, an, et quatenus abolitæ illæ sint, ventilator*. Herbornæ: Christophori Corvini, 1604.

———. *Politia Ecclesiastica: Sive, Forma, Ac Ratio Administrandi, Et Gubernandi Regni Christi, Quod Est Ecclesia in His Terris*. Herbonae: ex officina Christophori Corvini, 1607.

Zonaras, Johannes. *Ioannis Zonarae Monachi, qui olim Byzantij Magnus Drungarius excubiaru[m] seu Biglae, & protosecretarius fuit, Compendium historiarum*. Basel: Oporinus, 1557.

Zwinger, Theodore. *Theatrvm Hvmanae Vitae Theodori Zuingeri Bas[isliensis] Tertiatione. Nouem Volvminibvs locupletatum, interpolatum, renouatum. Cum tergemino Elencho, Methodi scilicet, Titulorum & Exemplorum*. Vol. 20. Basel: Episcopius, 1586.

SUBJECT INDEX

Abcoude, city of, 111ff
Abraham, 38
Adonis, 35fn89
Adriani, Cornelius, 96
Ahaz, King, 67Fn8
Aimoin of Fleury [Floriacensis Aimonius], 4–5, 13, 17, 58, 72, 79, 104
Aimonius, Floriacensis [Aimoin of Fleury], 4–5, 13, 17, 58, 72, 79, 104
Aix, city of, 12
Alaers, Franciscus, 95
Aldegonde, Lord van, 132
Alternatim singing, 7
Alting, Heinrich [Altingius], 72
Altingius, [Heinrich Alting], 72
Amalarius, 59
Ambrose of Milan, 54, 76, 92
Ames, William, 33
Andreæ, D. Jacob, 47, 72
Angilcus, Bartholomaeus, 30
Anglican Church, 48
Aphrodite, 51fn165
Apollo, 35fn86
Aquinas, Saint Thomas, 5, 18, 44, 45, 49, 51, 53, 59, 60, 65, 71, 105
Aristotle, 18, 49
Arsinoe II, Queen, 51fn165
Artemis, 35fn86

Aspilcueta, Martin [Navarre], 6, 40, 59, 60, 62, 71, 105
Athanasius, Bishop of Alexandria, 83
Athenaeus, 30–31, 54
Augsburg, Synod of, 105
Augustine, Saint Aurelius, 4, 44, 54, 59, 76, 77, 80, 82, 83, 84, 91, 93, 103
Aurillac, Gerbert of, 57
Aventinus, Johannes [Johann Georg Turmair], 11, 58

Bacchus, 35fn90
Bagpipe [instrument, Ultriculum], 29
Baile, Guillaume [Bayllius], 40
Baldric, Count, 4, 17
Bale, John [Baleus], 12, 61
Baleus [John Bale], 12, 61
Bardowick, city of, 126
Baronius, Caesar, 52, 60, 79, 84
Basil [Caesariensis Basilius], 52, 92
Basilius, Caesariensis [Basil], 52, 92
Batelier, Jacobus Johannes, 22
Bayllius [Guillaume Baile, John Bale], 12, 40, 61
Bell [instrument], 28, 43fn138, 51, 91, 111, 112
Bellarmine, Roberto Francesco Romolo, 17, 44, 50, 57, 62, 65, 79, 80
Bernard [Bernhardus], 13, 54, 81–82, 87
Bernhardus [Bernard], 13, 54, 81–82, 87
Bèza, Théodore de, 65, 76, 78

SUBJECT INDEX

Bochellus [Laurent Bouchel], 50, 79
Bordeaux, Council of, 80
Bouchel, Laurent [Bochellus], 50, 79
Boulenger, Jules-César [Julii Caesaris Bulengeri,], 31, 36, 51, 57
Bourges, Council of, 79
Boxtel, David van, 22
Bremen, city of, 96
Brenz, Johannes, 47
Bruges, city of, 96
Brusch, Kaspar [Bruschius], 13
Bruschius [Kaspar Brusch], 13
Bucer, Martin [Aretius Felinus], 85–86
Bucina [instrument], 28
Bulengeri, Julii Caesaris [Jules-César Boulenger], 31, 36, 51, 57

Cajetan, Tommaso de Vio, 7, 13, 17, 18, 39, 41–42, 45, 49, 50, 59, 60, 62, 65, 80, 89, 105
Calckman, Jan Jansz., 108ff
Calderwood, David, 66
Calvin, John, 70
Carpi, Prince of [Alberto Pio], 40, 56
Carthusian, Dionysius [Denis], 55–56
Castanets [instrument], 79
Champius, Jacobus Dale [Jacques Daléchamps], 31
Chapel Royal, 47
Charlemagne, 11
Choirs, 49
Christmas Day, 112
Chrysostom, John, 16–17, 52, 62, 78, 80, 83, 84
Cithara [instrument], 11, 28, 29, 51, 57, 74, 76, 79, 86, 90
Clavichord [instrument], 28
Clemens, Aurelius Prudentius, 78
Clemens, Titus Flavius [Clement of Alexandria], 62
Clement of Alexandria [Titus Flavius Clemens], 62
Clement VIII, Pope, 41fn125
Cologne, Council of, 105
Compiègne, city of, 5
Conch-shells [instrument], 31fn61
Constantine, 5

Constantinople, Sixth Council of, 54
Coppen, Bartholomaeus [Coppenius], 72
Coppenius [Bartholomaeus Coppen], 72
Copronymus, Constantine V, 58, 60, 61, 79
Cornu [instrument], 28
Crumhorn [instrument], 14
Ctesibius, 30–31, 51
Cudsemius, Petrus, 66
Cymbal [instrument], 28, 50, 51, 74, 78, 90, 123
Cyprian, 77

Daléchamps, Jacques [Jacobus Dale Champius], 31
Damasus, Pope, 104
Danaeus, Lambertus, 70
Dardanus, 84
David, King, 5, 10–11, 15, 16, 31, 34, 51, 60, 74, 84, 86, 89, 90
Democares, 105
Denis [Dionysius Carthusian], 55–56
Desmarets, Samuel [Samuel Maresius], 23
Dieu, Ludovicus de, 69
Dionysus, 15, 35fn87
Discantus, 55
Dordrecht, city of 95
Dordrecht, Synod of, 43, 73, 95, 129–130
Driesche, Johannes van den [Johannes Drusius], 37
Drusius, Johannes [Johannes van den Driesche], 37
Durand, Jean-Etienne [Ionnes Stephanu Durantis], 42, 45, 60, 103ff
Durant, William [Guilelmus Durantis], 5, 60
Durantis, Guilelmus [William Durand], 5, 60
Durantis, Ionnes Stephanu [Jean-Etienne Durand], 42, 45, 60, 103ff

Eckhard [Henricus Eckhardus], 46, 48, 67
Eckhardus, Henricus [Eckhard], 46, 48, 67
Egypt, 38
Einhardus, Hilduin, 11
Eprem Syrus [the Syrian], 78
Erasmus, Desiderius, 14–15, 18, 40, 72, 92

SUBJECT INDEX

Erpe, Thomas van [Thomo Erpino], 29
Erpino, Thomo [Thomas van Erpe], 29
Essenius, Andreas, 97ff
Estienne, Henri [Henry Stephano], 31
Eubulus, Christophilus [Jacobus
    Koelman], 128ff
Euripides, 50, fn161
Ezra, Rabbi Aben, 29

Faukeel, Hermannum [Hermannus
    Faukelius], 122ff, 132
Faukelius, Hermannus [Hermannum
    Faukeel], 122ff, 132
Felinus, Aretius [Martin Bucer], 86
Fibula, 85
Filesac, Jean, 57
Fischer, Johann [Johannes Piscator],
    71, 72
Fistula [instrument], 28
Floriacensis, Aimonus, 4–5
Flute [instrument], 18, 36–38, 45, 72, 125
Fortunatus, Amalarius, 104
Francken, Ægidius, 133ff
Frankfurt upon Oder, city of, 68
Franks, kingdom of, 17, 58
Fredericus, Prince of Orange Henricus,
    69
Frick, Christopher, 126
Frick, Kaspar, 126
Fullenius, Bernardus, 74
Fumus, Bartholomaeus, 39
Funerals, 37

Gad, prophet, 16
Gaul, Synod of, 79
Gelderland, Synod of, 132
Génébrard, Gilbert, 58
George of Venice [Gregory of Valencia],
    12, 17, 39, 59
Germany, 58
Glicas [Michael Glycas], 104
Golius, Jacobus, 69
Goutière, Jacques [Jacobus Gutherius], 36
Gregorian chant, 27
Groningen, city of, 68
Groot, Huigh de [Hugo Grotius], 37
Grotius, Hugo [Huigh de Groot], 37

Gutherius, Jacobus [Jacques Goutière], 36

Hague, city of, 114ff
Harp [instrument], 17 29, 49, 50, 72
Haymo, monk, 17
Hedylus, 51
Heidanus, Abrahamus, 69
Heidelberg, University of, 73
Heimenbergius, Ionnes [Johannes
    Heimenberg], 21ff, 69
Heinsius, Daniel, 69
Heusden, city of, 22, 73
Hezekiah, 16, 76
Hoornbeek, Johannes, 132
Horns [instrument], 18, 57, 72, 81
Hospiniano, Rodolpho [Rudolph Wirth],
    9ff, 59, 132
Huygens, Constantijn, 19ff, 69, 70, 86ff,
    92, 96, 108ff
Hydralus [hydraulicon, instrument],
    30, 51
Hymns, 35

Ioannettus, 104
Isaac, 38
Isidore [of Seville], 77, 86, 104

Jacob, 38
Jansen, Harmen, 107
Jarchi, Rabbi Solomon [Rashi], 29
Jerome, Saint, 54, 78, 81, 85, 104
John, Pope XXII, 56, 60
Josephus, Flavius, 10
Julianus, Flavius Claudius, 57, 104
Justin Martyr, 7, 11, 16, 44, 52, 62, 77, 81
Juvenal, 84

Kempis, Thomas á, 83
Kimchi, Rabbi David [Kimhi, Qimchi,
    RaDaK], 29
Knipperdolling, Bernhard, 118
Koelman, Jacobus [Christophilus
    Eubulus], 128ff
Krantz, Albrecht, 12

Lactanius, Lucius Coelius Firmianus, 14,
    18, 37, 73

SUBJECT INDEX

Langekruys, Jan van [Langhecrucius], 44
Langhecrusius [Jan van Langekruys], 44
Laodicea, Council of, 53
Lapide, Cornelius á [Cornelis Cornelissen van den Steen], 41
Larenus, 132
Lavater, Ludwig, 9
Levites, tribe of, 10, 16, 50, 74
Leyden, city of, 69
Lille, city of, 3
Lindanus, Guilelmus Damasus [Van der Lindt], 40, 50, 80
Lindt, van der [Guilelmus Damasus Lindanus], 40, 50, 80
Lorini, Jean de [Johannes Lorinus], 42, 57, 59
Lorinus, Johannes [Jean de Lorini], 42, 57, 59
Louis the Pious, King, 13, 17, 60, 105
Louvain, University of, 3
Louvain, Saint Peter's Church, 3
Lutheran faith, 33, 59
Lütkeschwager, Johannes [Johannes Micraelius], 59
Lydius, Balthasar the Elder, 94
Lyons, city of, 81
Lyre [instrument], 28, 36, 57, 78, 79

Maassluis, city of, 133
Madrigal, 27
Maimonides, 37
Manasses, Constantine, 104
Mantuanus, Baptista Spagnuoli [Mantvani Mantuanus], 12, 61
Mantuanus, Mantvani [Baptista Spagnuoli Mantuanus], 12, 61
Maresius, Samuel [Samuel Desmarets], 23
Maxwell, Bishop John, 48
Melanchton, Philip, 32
Meurius, Ionnis [Johannes van Meurs], 30
Meurs, Johannes, van [Ionnis Meurius], 30
Micraelius, Johannes [Johannes Lütkeschwager], 59
Middelburg, city of, 122, 131
Middelburg, Synod of, 43, 95, 132
Ministril [instrument], 45

Molanus, Johannes [Jan Vermeulen], 3ff, 60, 62
Momus, 92
Montbéliard, Colloquy of, 47, 65, 71
Motet, 27
Mouchy, Antoine de [antonion Monchiaceno Demochare Ressonaeo], 42
Musculus, Wolfgang, 70

Nablum [instrument], 11, 31, 74, 90
Nathan, prophet, 16, 76
Navarre [Martin Aspilcueta], 6, 40, 59, 60, 62, 71, 105
Nebrija, Antonio de [Antonius Nebrissensis], 37
Nebrissensis, Antonius [Antonio de Nebrija], 37
Nethenus, Matthias, 97ff
New Year's Day, 112

Opava, Martin of [Martin Pollonus], 104
Osiander, Andreas, 121ff

Pandura [instrument], 28
Pareus, David, 72
Parker, Robert, 33
Parresius, Theophilus [Jacobus Koelman], 128ff
Pepin, King, 5, 11, 58, 79, 104
Peraldus, Guillelmus, 56fn185
Périon, Joachim [Perionius], 77
Perionius [Joachim Périon], 28
Perkins, William [Perkinsus], 71
Perkinsus [William Perkins], 71
Pichius, 93
Pio, Alberto [Prince of Carpi], 40, 56
Piscator, Johannes [Johann Fischer], 72, 73
Plantina, Bartholomaeus, 12, 61, 104
Plato, 35
Pliny the Younger, 52, 76
Plutarch, 36
Pollonus, Martain [Martin of Opava], 104
Pollux, Iulius, 30
Polyander, Johannes, 69

SUBJECT INDEX

Polydore [Polydorus Vergilius], 10, 11, 57, 58
Possevino, Antonio [Possevinus], 78
Possevinus [Antonio Possevino], 78
Precentor [phonascus], 84
Pricaeus [John Price], 36
Price, John [Pricaeus], 36
Proclus, 35
Procopius of Gaza, 15, 16
Psaltery [psalteries], 17, 28, 93, 94

Rainolds, John [Rainoldus], 74
Reede, Johan van, 25
Renswoude, city of, 25
Ressonaeo, Antonio Monchiaceno Demochare [Antoine de Mouchy], 42
Rhodiginus [Lodovico Ricchieri], 104
Rhyton, 51
Rivet, André [Andreas Rivetus], 16ff, 65, 72, 80, 132
Rivetus, Andreas [André Rivet], 16ff, 65, 72, 80, 132
Rome, city of, 29
Rosary, 32

Sabellicus, Marcus Antonius Coccius, 13
Sackbut [instrument], 14
Salmasius, Claudius [Claude de Saumaise], 31
Sánchez, Tomás, 40
Saumaise, Claude de [Claudius Salmasius], 31
Schook, Martin, 68ff
Schotanus, Christian, 20
Schulting, Cornelius, 42
Schurman, Anna Maria van, 19
Scoti, Mariani [Marinus Scotus], 11, 58, 104
Scotus, Marinus [Mariani Scoti], 11, 58, 104
Sedan, University of, 73
Senonense, Council of, 5, 79
Shawm [instrument], 14
Shofar [instrument], 75
Sistrum [instrument], 28
Sixtus IV, Pope, 13

Sneek, city of, 106ff
Solomon, King, 5, 60
Soto, Domingo de, 105
South Holland, Synod of, 86
Steen, Cornelis Cornelissen van den [Cornelius á Lapide], 41
Stephano, Henry [Henrico Stephano, Henri Estienne], 31, 59
Suarez, Francisco, 41, 49, 57, 60
Sylvester II, Pope, 57–58

Talculf of Thuringia, 5
Tambourine [instrument], 29
Tertullian Quintus Septimius Florens, 52, 36–37, 76–77
Theater, 36
Theophilos of Byzantium, 13fn13, 104
Theophylactus, 83
Tibia [instrument], 28
Tilenus, Daniel, 65–66
Torre, Raphael de la [Francisco de Turrianus], 44
Trajan, Emperor, 76
Trent, Council of, 8, 40, 105
Trumpet [instrument], 14, 18, 37, 50, 51, 57, 72, 78, 81, 91
Tuba [instrument], 28
Turmair, Johann Georg [Johannes Aventinus], 11, 58
Turrianus, Francisco de [Raphael de la Torre], 44
Tympanum [instrument], 28

Ultriculum [instrument, bagpipe], 29
Ussher, James [Usserius], 74
Utrecht, city of, 22ff, 64ff, 68, 97ff, 113

Valencia, Gregory of [George of Venice], 17, 39, 59, 62
Velde, Abraham van de, 131ff
Venus, 51fn165
Vergile, Polydore [Vergilius], 10, 31, 57, 58
Vergilius, Polydorus [Vergile], 10, 31, 57, 58
Vermigli, Peter Martyr, 75, 132
Vermuelen, Jan [Johannes Molanus], 3ff

SUBJECT INDEX

Viguerus [Jean Viguier], 39
Viguier, Jean [Viguerus], 39
Vitalian, Pope, 12, 17, 60, 61, 80, 94–95, 104
Vitruvius, Marcus, 4
Voetius, Gisbertus, 19ff, 21ff, 68ff, 97ff
Vorstius, Adolphus, 69

Whitgift, John [Johann Whitgistus], 47
Whitgistus, Johann [John Whitgift], 47

Wirth, Rudolph [Rodolpho Hospiniano], 9ff
Wyn, Govert van, 133–134

Yehunda, Rabbi, 36

Zephyr, Temple of, 51
Zepper, Wilhelm, 43, 51, 51fn165, 65, 73, 87
Zonaras, Johannes, 13
Zurich, city of, 9

SCRIPTURE INDEX

Genesis
      4, 29, 30
4:21   29

Exodus
      15, 42, 51
15:12   132
28:34–35   50, 90
32   26

Leviticus
19:28   38
25:9   90

Numbers
10:2–3   90
19:1–2   74

I Samuel
16:24   124

II Samuel
23:1   74

II Kings
3:15   124
4   15
16:10–18   67fn8

I Chronicles
6:31,   74
      25, 36
25:1   74
25:1–5   28
25:1–6   50, 90

II Chronicles
4:22   27
5:12–13   28
29:25   16, 74, 75

Ezra
3:10–11   74

Nehemiah
12:24   75

Job
      93
21:12   29
30:21   29

Psalm
32   44
33   62, 73, 85
35   83
45   132
46   80
47:8   82

SCRIPTURE INDEX

Psalm (continued)

56	59, 103
57:8	34
57:8–9	81
56:8 [57:7]	34fn81
69	83
71:22–234	81
109	83
119:99–100	75
150	3, 16, 29, 30, 62, 123
150:3–4	133ff
150:4	29

Isaiah

8	52
29:13	82fn37

Jeremiah

9:17	37fn105, 38

Ezekiel

33:32	29

Daniel

3	28

Amos

6:5	27

Matthew

7:26	109
9:23	36–37
15	32
15:8	83
18	33

Luke

9:55	83
22:48	110

I Corinthians

7–16	49
8	33
10	33
10:31	34
11:22	124
14	14, 18, 23fn6, 40, 41, 62, 70, 72, 75, 81, 82, 89
14:7	27–28, 70
14:7–8	36
14:12–26	49, 89
14:15	75, 82
14:16	99
14:19	96
14:26	99, 132
14:40	75, 88
16:7	44

II Corinthians

1:15	83
6:15	109

Galatians

4:9	51

Ephesians

4:29	83
5	76, 78, 80, 81
5:18–19	75
5:19	54, 72, 83

Colossians

2	32
2:23	39
3	78, 81, 83
3:15–17	51
3:16	72, 75, 82

II Thessalonians

2:16	83

I Timothy

	83

SCRIPTURE INDEX

James
5:13 — 75

I Peter
1:8 — 49
2:3 — 49
4:3 — 91

Wisdom
19:17 — 57, 59

Sirach
32 — 42

www.ingramcontent.com/pod-product-compliance
Lightning Source LLC
Chambersburg PA
CBHW022123160426
43197CB00009B/1128